The Musée national du Moyen Age
Thermes de Cluny

Hôtel de Cluny,
6, place Paul Painlevé 75005 Paris
Open every day, except Tuesday,
from 9.15 a.m. to 17.45 p.m.
Tel. (1) 53 73 78 00
Fax (1) 43 25 85 27

MUSÉES ET MONUMENTS DE FRANCE
COLLECTION DIRECTED BY PIERRE LEMOINE

The Musée national du Moyen Age

Thermes de Cluny

Viviane Huchard
Chief Curator

Elisabeth Antoine
Sophie Lagabrielle
Pierre-Yves Le Pogam
Curators

Fondation Paribas
Réunion des Musées Nationaux

Acknowledgements

We should like to thank the Museum's donors, of whom we can here name only all-too-small a number. Through their generosity they have enriched the collections and helped ensure that they have flourished.

Charles Sauvageot, 1849
Arthur Forgeais, 1852
Emile Boeswillwald, 1853
Henry Leroy, 1854
Achille Jubinal, 1860
Benjamin Fillon, 1867
Eugène Piot, 1870
Emile Cottenot, 1873
Louis A. J. Gérard, 1877
Fabien Lambert, 1880
Charles Timbal, 1881
Jules Audéoud, 1885
Edouard de Beaumont, 1888
Frédéric Moreau, 1889
Baron Adolphe de Rothschild, 1889
Charles Piet-Lataudrie, 1890
Baroness Nathaniel de Rothschild, 1890
Alfred d'Affry de la Monnoye, 1893
Stanislas Baron, 1897
Achille-François Wasset, 1897
Jules Ravel, 1899
Charles Rochard, 1903
Isaac and Moïse de Camondo, 1910
David David-Weill, 1928
Edmond Dollfuss, 1930
Jean-Joseph Marquet de Vasselot, 1930
Marcel Guérin, 1934
Claudius Côte, 1961
Henri Seyrig, 1961
Pauline and Clotilde Bacri, 1972
Banque Française du Commerce Extérieur, 1980
Jean Boxhorn, 1981
Guy Ladrière, 1987
Pierre and Nicole Verlet, 1988
André Matossian, 1993

Thanks are due to all those who have helped produce this book: Marie-Thérèse Augé, Anita Dret, Sophie Fiblec-Rochard, Vincent Hildebert, Christine Lancestremère, Katherine Martinet, Odile Menegaux, Jean-Christophe Ton-That. Thanks must also go to all the Museum staff. We hope that they will find cause for pride in the pages that follow.

Cover:
'Leopard Embroidery',
1st third 14th century, detail
(see ill. 118)

Half title:
Main courtyard of the Hôtel de Cluny
Lithograph from *Les Arts au Moyen Age*
by Alexandre Du Sommerard, Paris,
1834

Frontispiece:
Saint James Major as a Pilgrim
Burgundy, end 15th century
Stone

Page 3:
Four partridges
Normandy, *c.* 1500
Stained glass

Front flap:
Figures brandishing weapons,
8th century (see ill. 20)

Preface

The Musée National du Moyen Age occupies a special position amongst French national museums. Not only is it famed for the quality and rarity of its collections, but it is also in itself a remarkable monument, located in the heart of the Quartier Latin and combining two separate buildings of quite different design and character. The older of these is the Gallo-Roman bath-house, dating from the first century AD; and the more recent is the late fifteenth-century mansion-house that was previously the Paris residence of the abbots of Cluny.

The Museum was created in 1843, at the height of the Romantic period. It owes its existence to the enthusiasm of the collector Alexandre Du Sommerard (1779–1842) and to the desire of the French nation to learn more about its history. As the years passed, a number of spectacular acquisitions, such as the *Lady and the Unicorn* tapestries and the remains of the treasure from Basle cathedral, conferred an aura of prestige on the collections.

Because of the way in which the exhibits are presented, both inside the building and in the gardens, the intimate ambience and unique character of the place have remained unspoiled, and this has brought the Museum international regard. Since 1946, the main medieval strand in the collections has been reinforced: monumental fragments from Notre-Dame in Paris, from the abbey of Saint-Denis, and from the Sainte-Chapelle, as well as various objects from everyday life join together with precious items in silver, gold, and ivory to provide a unique account of the history of medieval art.

As it prepares for renovation, it seems appropriate to remind as wide an audience as possible of the riches that lie hidden within the Museum, now over a century old. In this connection, we are extremely grateful for the unstinting support of the Fondation Paribas, which will include the present volume in its prestigious series *Musées et Monuments de France.*

The selection of works to be included in this survey was made by the keepers of the Museum, and it proved to be a difficult one, given the hundreds of items – out of many thousands – which competed for inclusion. In the end, over 160 works were retained, and these are here considered as part of a general survey of the history of art, in which a mixture of thematic, artistic, and technical aspects are considered. With its wealth of fine illustrations, the book forms part of the Museum's overall scheme of renovation: the Museum is open to a very broad public, and its mission is to familiarize people with the Middle Ages through the artistic, technical, and cultural output of that time; publications such as the present one make a major contribution to that mission, and we hope that this book will provide visitors with guidance and with new opportunities for instruction and delectation.

Viviane Huchard, Chief Curator

The History of the Museum

The Musée National du Moyen Age is one of the great national museums of France in which the exhibits and the buildings are as exceptional as one another. When it was founded in 1843, the Museum combined two structures of differing character and purpose: the Gallo-Roman baths, built during the first century, and the Paris residence of the abbots of Cluny. *1*

The Roman Baths

The Thermes du Nord or Northern Baths, known as the Cluny Baths, are the most imposing and best-preserved Gallo-Roman remains north of the Loire. Built in the first century, they were the main baths in Lutetia and continued to be used until the end of the third century. They were part of an administrative and trading centre built on one of the hills (now known as Mount Sainte-Geneviève) which overlooked the Seine. Originally, the buildings formed a huge rectangle measuring at least 100 metres by 65. Although they are now partly in ruins, their capacity and height, the structure of the *frigidarium* (cooling-room) – which has survived intact – and the extent of the basement area all testify to the vision and boldness of the Roman builders.

The fact that the *frigidarium* has remained in constant use has ensured its preservation. (During the seventeenth century it housed a cooper's workshop, documented in detail in a painting by Hubert Robert.) The groin vaults remain intact, measuring about 15 metres at their highest point. They rest on consoles carved in the shape of ships' prows – a feature which has been taken to indicate involvement by the powerful guild of Paris Boatmen, the *Nautes*, in the baths' construction. The walls, built of small quarry-stones separated by brick courses, were originally clad in marble, stucco, or mosaic. *2*

2 Mosaic depicting Cupid astride a dolphin
Probably originally located in the Baths, late 2nd–early 3rd century

Unearthed in the mid-nineteenth century, in the course of roadworks and as part of the scheme to incorporate them into the Museum, the baths were investigated by Théodore Vacquer, the municipal architect. After the Second World War, major excavations exposed the building's basic layout. Further excavations took place between 1990 and 1993, revealing a highly elaborate structure. All the walls at the lower level have survived intact and provide a complete picture of the changing use of the building between the first and third centuries.

The excellently preserved *frigidarium* and the tepid or cold rooms lie within the Museum; the *caldarium* (bath-room), *caldarium-frigidarium,* and one of the *palaestrae* (gymnasiums), with large parts of their walls intact, lie outside the building. Hypocausts, conduits, fragments of flooring, and the floor-covering in the basement all indicate the imposing scale of the building.

1 Main courtyard of the Hôtel de Cluny

3 View of the *frigidarium* by Etienne Bouhot, 1845: display of the collection of antique and medieval stonework

4 View of the *frigidarium* in its present condition with the statue of the Emperor Julian the Apostate, installed in 1937

The Hôtel de Cluny

In the thirteenth century, the powerful abbots of Cluny in Burgundy bought a number of houses opposite the recently founded university in Paris. These occupied a site backing onto the Roman baths, with use of a hanging garden over the vaults of the *frigidarium*. At the end of the fifteenth century, Jacques d'Amboise, whose brothers distinguished themselves by their generous patronage of the arts, had a new mansion built here. This was intended for private use, and its size, arrangement, and refined Flamboyant Gothic decoration all betokened the lavish life-style of a *grand seigneur* of the late Middle Ages. *4*

Built in a U-shape, the mansion has a long wing with two small right-angled extensions marking off a trapezoidal courtyard edged by a crenellated wall. The building has several spiral staircases; the largest of these, jutting out onto the main courtyard, bears the arms of the builder, Jacques d'Amboise. On the north side, along which runs a now unplanted garden, there is another wing housing a two-storeyed chapel. The vaulting on the first floor is a remarkable example of Flamboyant Gothic at its apogee. The Hôtel de Cluny, the first private mansion with a courtyard and garden in Paris, is remarkably well preserved, both internally and externally. *1*

5 Alexandre Du Sommerard (1779–1842). Lithograph by Achille Devéria, *c.* 1835

The Collections

The creation of the Museum came about as a result of two events. The first was the acquisition by the State, in 1843, of the collections belonging to Alexandre Du Sommerard, together with the mansion in which they were housed; and the second was the donation, by the City of Paris, of the Gallo-Roman baths, containing various classical and medieval sculptures. These dual origins have determined the Museum's choice of focus.

Alexandre Du Sommerard was one of the most colourful figures in the art-collecting world of the Romantic period. He was born in 1779 and may have acquired his taste for antiquities during his stay in Italy at the time of Bonaparte's campaign. After this, he made a creditable career at the Cour des Comptes, and in 1831 became a *conseiller-maître*. By nature jovial and inquisitive, he sought the company of others, moved in artistic and lettered circles, and took part in the activities of historical societies working to safeguard monuments and documents relating to national history. Inspired by the memory of the Musée des Monuments Français, created by Alexandre Lenoir in the Austin friary after the Revolution, many collectors – Carrand, Debruge-Duménil, Révoil, Sauvageot, Willemin, Denon – were now setting up cabinets of curiosities. Du Sommerard likewise assembled a collection of objects, and in 1832 he decided to install them in the Hôtel de Cluny, part of which was let to him by a printer. He set up, and then exhibited, his growing collection in one half of the first floor, where the chapel was located. 'He would present his collection in an exquisitely polite fashion; and, without any hint of the lecturer about him, he would deliver lessons in practical archeology which captured one's interest and which one never forgot', says Prosper Mérimée. Achille Devéria painted a picture of Du Sommerard as part of his famous set of portraits of contemporary figures. Exploiting the magnificent context of the mansion-house, Sommerard evoked the memory of various great men. François I was the object of especial glorification: a whole room was devoted to him, and his bed, stirrups and *5* *7* various other objects rather generously attributed to him were on view. Sommerard made use of the fact that the chapel was arranged on two levels to separate out items relating to religious worship. Elsewhere, styles and periods were mixed, and the most disparate objects were placed alongside one another, with no real concern for chronology.

When Sommerard died in 1842, his contemporaries, sensitive to the links that were growing up between the collection and the building, sought to make these permanent by creating a museum. The project had gained impetus in 1836, when the City of Paris installed its stonework collection,

6 Edmond Du Sommerard (1817–1885). Photograph by Carjat, *c.* 1860

7 View of the chapel Lithograph from *Les Arts au Moyen Age* by Alexandre Du Sommerard, Paris, 1834

including a great many sculptures from demolition sites and restoration *3* projects in Paris, and also from excavations, in the *frigidarium*. A law of 1844 approved the creation of 'a museum devoted especially to the monuments, furnishings, and precious objects from Antiquity, the Middle Ages, and the Renaissance'. The City of Paris made the baths and stonework collection over to the State, and the latter purchased the mansion-house and Alexandre Du Sommerard's collection. The combination of the two collections conferred a unique character on the Museum's astonishingly diverse holdings.

8 As early as 1833, the architect Albert Lenoir, son of the founder of the Musée des Monuments Français, had put forward plans for a 'historical museum combining the Roman baths and the Cluny mansion-house'.

When the Museum was set up, he was therefore, quite naturally, asked to take on the task of restoring the mansion and putting in hand the work needed for its conversion, in collaboration with its director. In 1844, Edmond Du Sommerard, son of the collector, was appointed curator. *6* The Museum was an instant success. The forty years during which Edmond Du Sommerard oversaw the collections were particularly felicitous ones, and served only to increase public interest in the Museum. By the time he died (in 1885), the collections had grown enormously. But the intimate atmosphere created by Alexandre Du Sommerard had changed little. The gardens, adorned with monumental sculptures, now formed part of the display. Thanks to his good relations within the Commission des Monuments Historiques, Edmond Du Sommerard was able to secure a good many masterpieces for the Museum: the Apostles from the Sainte-Chapelle, the tapestries of *Seigneurial Life*, the famous *Lady and the Unicorn* series, and the equally sumptuous one of *David and Bathsheba* (now in the Musée National de la Renaissance at Ecouen). He also added some unique items of goldsmith's work to the Museum's holdings, including the crowns of the Visigoth kings and various rare pieces from the treasury of Basle cathedral. The prestige of the Museum was such that a host of similar establishments were set up – the Bayerisches Museum in Munich, for example, and the Schnütgen Museum in Cologne.

Until the Second World War, the Museum, although steadily building up its holdings in the various sections, retained its nineteenth-century appearance. Its reopening in 1946 marked the start of a new phase: major structural works had to be put in hand, and the collections were reorganized and presented in a new way. The Roman baths were used to display a small number of antique sculptures, and the various rooms of the mansion now accommodated the *objets d'art* and historical items from the medieval period. The museographical selection which this reorganization entailed meant that a new museum – the Musée de la Renaissance – could be set up at Ecouen, and that other museums could enrich their own holdings with deposits from Cluny. The Museum hopes that further renovation work will help it to become even more effective in its task of familiarizing the public with the Middle Ages. To show respect for, and conserve, the buildings in which it is housed, to reorganize the collections in line with contemporary museological thinking, and to improve conditions for its ever more numerous and ever more enquiring visitors – these are the principles that guide the Museum in its undertaking. And in order to succeed, that undertaking is dependent on the support of the relevant departments – of archeology, architecture, and heritage – within the Ministry of Culture.

V.H.

8 The architect Albert Lenoir (1801–1891). Bronze medallion by Antoine Etex

The First Millennium

For a long time, history traditionally regarded the year 476 as marking a watershed in the West's first millennium. On one side of this date came the rise and fall of the Roman empire, on the other the first five 'dark' centuries of the Middle Ages. In fact, 476 (the date of the deposition of the last head of the Western Roman empire) is not particularly significant. Taking a long-term view, one would tend nowadays to see the whole flux of events from about 300 (the reign of Constantine) up to the year 1000 – in other words, late Antiquity to the Ottonian empire, by way of the barbarian kingdoms and the Carolingian empire – as a single, albeit multifaceted, block. Such a view gives a clearer account of, in particular, the interaction between the Byzantine world, Islam, and the barbarian kingdoms via their late classical roots and common heritage.

10 Ingot from Saint-Marc-le-Blanc
Western France, 9th–6th century BC
Gold

Torc
Gaul, 3rd–1st century BC
Gold

The first three centuries of the present age, on the other hand, obviously present quite a different picture: that of a unified Roman empire, pagan in its beliefs, and utterly, or very nearly, unassailed. And yet, when considering medieval civilization, it is useful to take elements of classical art – Roman and provincial – into account, because they contain the dual seed from which the medieval aesthetic sprang. These were, on the one hand, the genius of Greco-Roman art, and, on the other, the provincial currents, which, as well as picking up on pre-Roman (notably Celtic) strands in the populations conquered and assimilated by Rome, also chime in with the anti-classical trends that were later to be introduced by the Germanic peoples.

9 Book board depicting Saint Paul
Echternach (?), 2nd quarter
11th century
Ivory

From the Celtic period, the Museum owns a small number of examples of goldsmith's work illustrating the creativity and technical skill of Gallic *10* artists in this field. An ingot and torc, both of gold, prove that this kind of art was practised during the Hallstatt and La Tène periods. However, the conquest of south-east Gaul in 121 BC, and that of the rest of Gaul by Julius Caesar, brought gradual absorption into Roman civilization. In Lutetia, as elsewhere, the local élites adopted the customs and institutions of the capital, bringing innovations that ranged from the habit of visiting sumptuous public baths to a gradual shift in native religion towards syncretic forms. An excellent illustration of this is provided by sec- *11* tions from a monumental pillar discovered under the choir of Notre-Dame in Paris during the eighteenth century. The pillar, which was

11 *Nautes* (Paris boatmen) Pillar: *Esus and Cernunnos* (details)
Paris, AD 14–37
Stone

intended to carry a statue of Jupiter, was dedicated to the Emperor Tiberius by the Paris boatmen – the same ones who probably commissioned the Cluny Baths. Great Gallic gods were depicted on the pillar, alongside (not amalgamated with) the chief divinities of the Greco-Roman pantheon, and we thus have a record – in parts unique – of these gods' names and iconography. Clearly, at the start of the first century, the Romanization of Gaul was only just getting under way.

During the *pax romana* of the first and second centuries, however, Gaul became one of the most prosperous and loyal provinces of the Roman empire. After the upheavals of the third century, Lutetia was even chosen, *12* for a very short time, as imperial capital by the Emperor Julian (361–3). Whereas his predecessor, Constantine, had given the stamp of approval to Christianity, Julian attempted to revive the old values of Roman paganism – hence his apparel, with its borrowings from the ancient philosophers and priests, and hence also the epithet 'Apostate' conferred on him by the Christians. At the end of the fourth century, however, the Emperor Theodosius made Christianity the official religion of the empire. Paganism nevertheless persisted amongst the senatorial aristocracy, as is *13* shown by a wing from a diptych bearing the name of the Nicomachi. The other panel, inscribed with the name of the Symmachi, is preserved in the Victoria and Albert Museum in London. The ivory diptych, itself very

12 *Emperor Julian the Apostate*
Roman empire, 2nd half
4th century
Stone

13 Wing of a diptych of the Nicomachi
and Symmachi families
Rome (?), *c.* AD 400
Ivory

14 Wing of a diptych of
the consul Areobindus
Constantinople, AD 506
Ivory

15 *Appliqué* ornament depicting
Ariadne and her retinue
Constantinople, early 6th century
Ivory

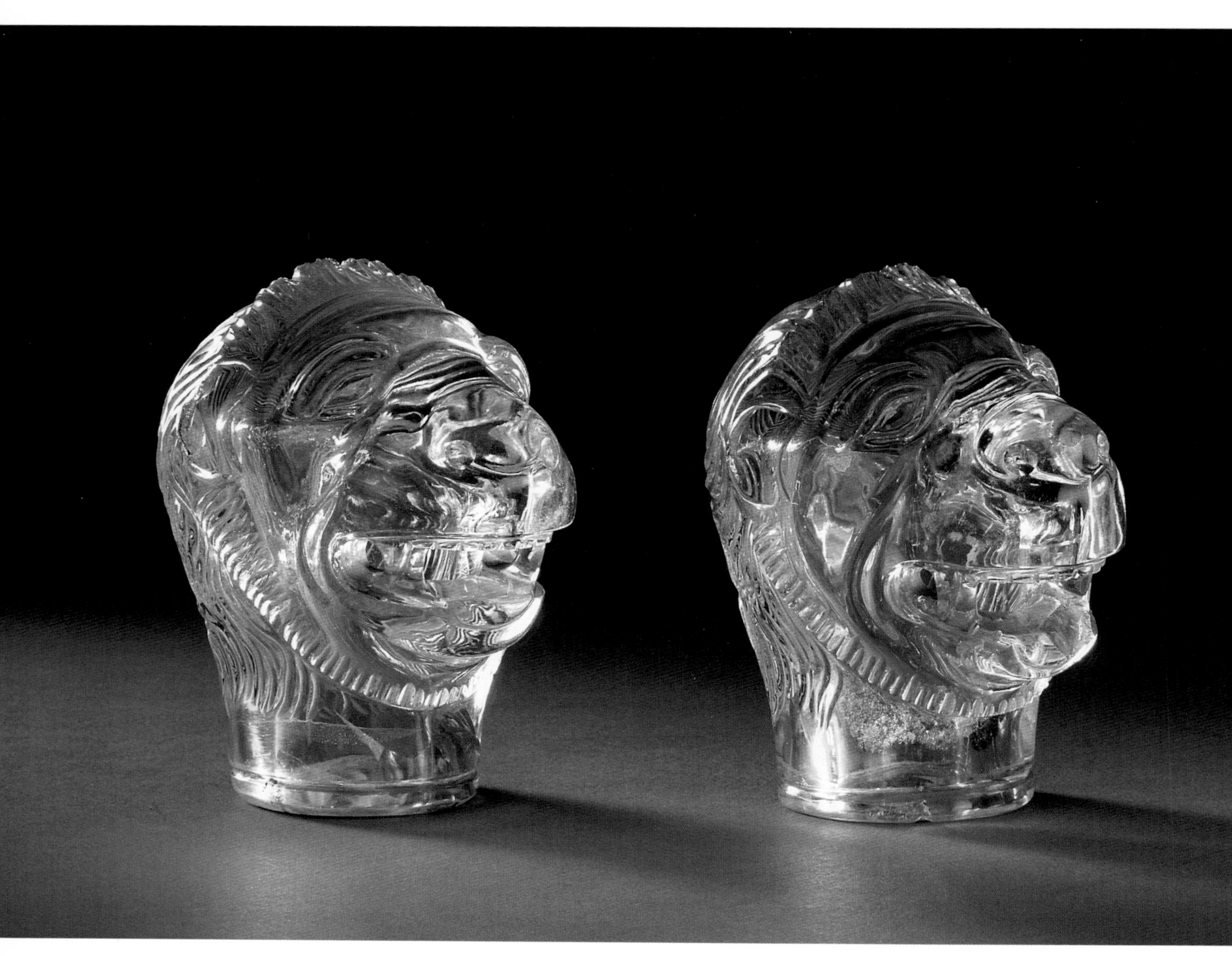

16 Lions' heads
Roman empire, 4th–6th century
Rock crystal

classical in execution, reflects the continuing attachment of these two high-born families to the traditional Roman pantheon (the panel in the Museum depicts a priestess of Ceres performing a rite to Cybele). By a strange twist of fate, this 'manifesto of moribund paganism' managed to survive because it was incorporated into a medieval reliquary.

The Byzantine Empire: Art at Court and in the Provinces

At the start of the sixth century, not only had paganism waned, but the Roman empire, split into two since the fourth century, had lost its Western half. Rome was no longer in Rome but in Constantinople (Byzantium), the capital of the Eastern empire. The latter – which was to last a thousand years, until Byzantium was captured by the Turks in 1453 and renamed Istanbul – thus came into being under Christian auspices. But it did not renounce its classical heritage. The office of consul, for example, though bereft of political significance, continued to exist, and provided an opportunity for the emperor to reward his relatives and close associates. Two lions' heads in rock crystal were formerly thought to *16* have been adornments for an imperial or consular throne. Although it is now clear that they should be seen in a broader context (perhaps as decorations for the throne of some oriental divinity), they retain their fascination on account of the material of which they are made and the stylized, three-dimensional treatment of the lions' faces. When he took office, the new consul would distribute ivory diptychs whose lavishness varied according to the rank of the recipient. A wing from a diptych of *14* the Consul Areobindus (the other wing probably resembled the ones preserved at Besançon, Lucca, and Zurich), shows the seated consul giving the signal for the circus games. Despite obvious continuity with the past glories of Rome, the jagged, almost clumsy script of the consul's title contrasts with the majestic lettering on the Nicomachi wing. Again, one is astounded to think that the fine figure of Ariadne, which probably *15* formed the upright of a seat or bed, with a matching Bacchus on the other side, was made as a prestigious commission in a profoundly Christian context. It should be remembered, however, that because of their association with wine, Dionysus and his companion were often linked with the Eucharistic mystery; and the aesthetic qualities of the figure, all curves and softness, are, in any case, far removed from the canons of classical beauty.

Far fewer examples of less durable materials, particularly textiles, have survived – except in Egypt, where the desert climate ensured that large numbers of everyday items were preserved. The Coptic civilization – the name given to Egyptian Christianity – was actually only one provincial variant of the late classical civilization that flourished on the edges of the Mediterranean; because almost all other evidence has disappeared, however, it provides the finest testimony we have of that culture. The textiles from that area were unearthed at the end of the nineteenth century, using excavation techniques that were unfortunately very rough and ready. As a result, much information, including even the provenance and date of some of the finds, was irrevocably lost. In most cases, therefore, classification is based on purely stylistic criteria. Despite this, the items concerned create a fascinating impression, giving some idea of the impact which the more official and prestigious output of the capitals and the court may have had. One also sees the gradual emergence of Christian themes, though these do not completely oust classical mythology,

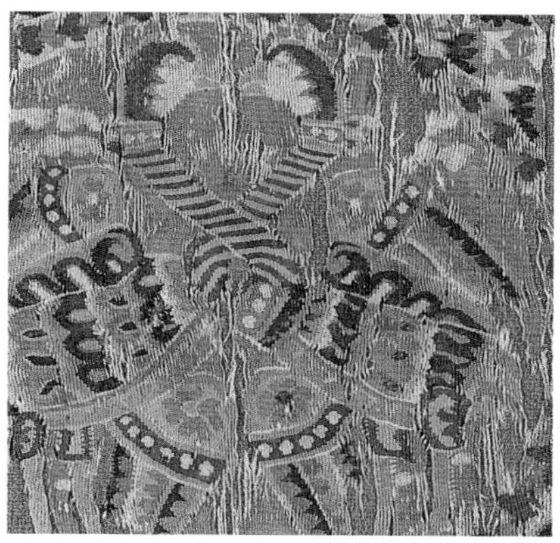

17 Quail
Coptic Egypt,
4th–5th century
Tapestry in wool and linen

18 Front-to-front birds
Coptic Egypt,
10th–11th century
Tapestry in wool

which may be used either with cryptic Christian significance or for purely decorative purposes. But it is especially in the enduring floral and faunal motifs (quail, front-to-front bird-figures, scrolls of foliage inhab-
17, 18, 21 ited by animals) that the development of a new aesthetic, diametrically opposed to that of classical art, is perceptible. Its main features are a reduction in volume and perspective, the advent of plain, sharply contrasting colours in place of gradation and nuance, the primacy of line and decorative effect over verisimilitude and naturalism, and the substitution
20 of symbol for representation. A frieze of figures brandishing weapons, for

19 Quadriga
Constantinople, *c.* 800
Silk

example, far from struggling to contain itself within a classical tradition which the artist was neither willing nor able to adopt, proclaims creative freedom with a dynamism reminiscent of contemporary art. This kind of work marks the birth of medieval art, which always both assimilated and moved beyond – in other words transformed – the past.

These radical changes were eventually also to make themselves felt at the heart of the Eastern empire. In the workshops of the capital, occupied mainly with court commissions, craftsmen of every speciality produced luxury objects reflecting the same aesthetic approach, although perhaps with more gravitas – and less humour – than the Egyptian workshops.
19 The Quadriga Silk is a good example. It consisted of a series of medallions with figures of ibexes in between – a reminder of the continuing influence of the Orient on Byzantine art. In the middle of each medallion was a scene depicting a triumph at the races (the inhabitants of Constantinople were extremely keen on these kinds of equestrian events). But the Museum owns only a fragment of the silk. The secondary figures (the charioteer's helpers and the servants distributing the prize money) are full of movement, in contrast to the static figure of the auriga with his four horses, arranged in an unlikely symmetrical frieze. The silk comes from the treasury at Aachen cathedral. It probably dates from about

20 Tapestry fragment depicting figures brandishing weapons, 8th century
Tapestry in linen and wool

21 Rinceau inhabited by animals
Coptic Egypt, 5th–6th century
Tapestry in wool and linen

22 Fragment of shroud from Saint-Sernin, Toulouse
Spain, 12th century
Silk

800, when there was a great deal of contact between the Byzantine and the new Western empire, refounded by Charlemagne.

During this time, Mohammed's teaching had brought about an apparently profound dichotomy in the Mediterranean region. After the hegira (622), which marked the start of a new era for Muslim believers, the prophet's message was supposed to lead not only to massive political changes in the whole area, but also to the inauguration of a new civilization based on the Koran. And yet, under the influence of the dynasts of Syria, Mesopotamia, Egypt, and elsewhere, aspects of the late classical legacy were absorbed, as is demonstrated by the religious architecture and the luxurious life-style of the courts. Likewise, the continual contact with the Christian world, notably Spain and Italy, led to a mutual enrichment of the two civilizations. The Peacock Silk, for example, which *22* contained the relics of Saint Exuperius at the church of Saint-Sernin in Toulouse, is a magnificent piece of work produced in Muslim-ruled twelfth-century Spain.

From the Barbarian Kingdoms to the Carolingian and Ottonian Empires

The West, meanwhile, was experiencing more turbulent times. The barbarian raids of the third and fourth centuries gradually turned into migratory flows of Germanic peoples who, whilst dividing up the spoils of the Roman empire and founding rival kingdoms, nevertheless considered themselves the legitimate heirs of that empire. The Visigoths, for example, who became powerful first in the south-west of France and later, more especially, in Spain, adopted the eagle as a motif in their *fibulae*. *25* The most prestigious Visigoth items in the collection, however, are the three votive crowns discovered during the nineteenth century at *26* Guarrazar, not far from the former Visigoth capital, Toledo, where they were probably hidden when the Muslims first invaded Spain (in 711). Made of gold and decorated with precious stones, they probably reflect the style of the insignia of the imperial court at Byzantium, which was taken as a model by all the Western kingdoms. In Gaul as well, the goldsmith's skill was displayed in items of great luxury. One such is a Frankish sword found in the Seine. *23* But Clovis's prestige and that of his successors derived mainly from his early conversion to Catholicism (most of the barbarian chiefs were Arianists). A sixth-century liturgical strainer, *24* which may have belonged to Saint Aubin of Angers, is a token of this crucial alliance between the Gallo-Roman Church and the Merovingian dynasty.

It fell to Charlemagne to reunite the Western world by bringing together territories that had been divided by the barbarian invasions, and by agreeing to be crowned emperor in Rome in the year 800. Of course, it was the classical heritage, notably in literature and art, that Charlemagne's court sought to revive via the empire. A diptych probably made *31* in Italy in about 900, using a carved object produced at some prior date in the Anglo-Saxon area, is a kind of continuation of the tradition of the consular diptych; but its prime reference, through its opulent scrolls of foliage peopled with centaurs and satyrs, is classical mythology – or the Christian interpretation of it. From this time on, despite various hiatuses and divisions, the notion of empire was to exert a continual influence on the course of European history. The last Carolingian emperor, for example, was deposed in 888, but as early as 962 a Germanic princely family

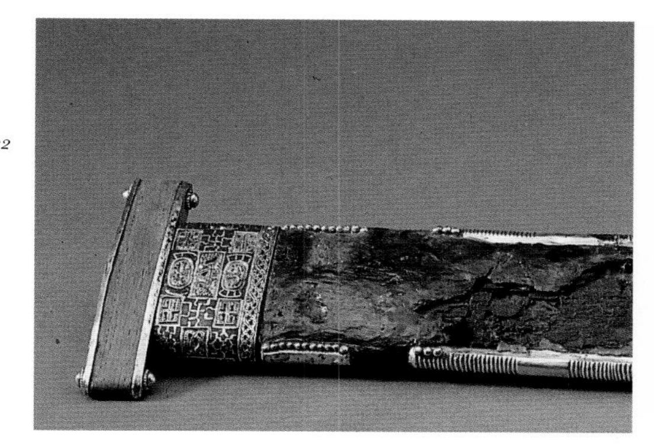

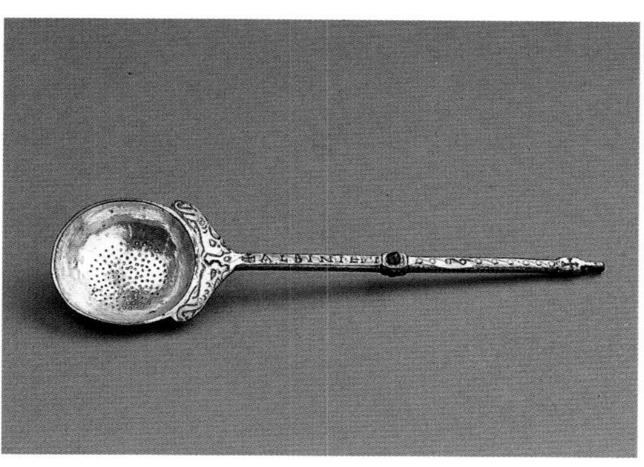

23 Fragment of a ceremonial sword and its scabbard
Gaul, 6th–7th century (?)
Wood, gold, copper

24 Liturgical strainer
Gaul, 6th century
Silver, niello, garnets

25 Pair of eagle-shaped *fibulae*
Visigothic (Castelsagrat), 6th century
Plate-buckle
Visigothic (Tressan), 1st half 6th century
Bronze

26 Votive crown found at Guarazzar,
inscribed 'Sonnica'
Visigoth Spain, 7th century
Gold and precious stones

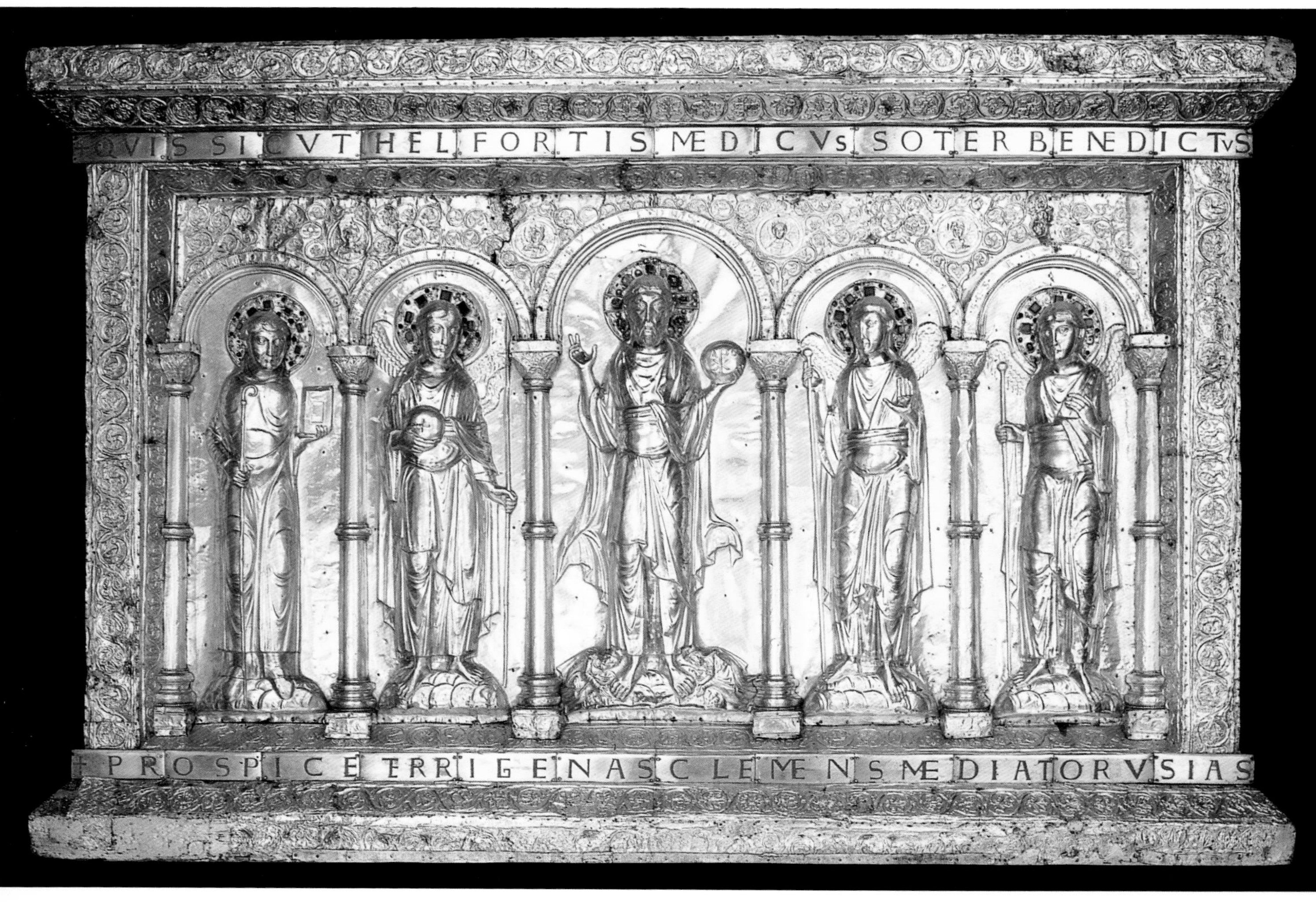

27 Altar-frontal from Basle cathedral
Bamberg (?), early 11th century
Gold

revived the dream of imperial grandeur by founding the Holy Roman Empire of the German Nation. This latter empire sought, moreover, to reappropriate some of the prestige of the Constantinople court. In 972, for instance, the Emperor Otto II married a Byzantine princess, Theophanu. The union is depicted on an ivory carving, probably made in the *29* German empire but perhaps by a Byzantine artist – or at least an artist strongly influenced by Byzantine models. Its composition is the same as that of an ivory depicting an imperial Byzantine couple (probably Romanus and Eudoxia) now in the Cabinet des Médailles at the Bibliothèque Nationale, Paris. But Ottonian art was not merely a repetition of Carolingian antecedents or oriental models. In a gold altar-frontal from *27* Basle cathedral (but made for another religious centre, perhaps Bamberg), the Emperor Heinrich II is pictured prostrate before Christ, in a typically Byzantine attitude of adoration; at the same time, Saint Benedict, father of Western monasticism, is figured amongst the archangels, almost on an equal footing. At the start of the eleventh century, the artistic centres of the Ottonian empire were diverse in character, and reflected the ambition and wealth of the various great German prelates. A figure of Saint Paul, with an intense, almost fierce, expression, gives us a *9* taste of the original and unforgettable style of a master ivory-carver probably based in Echternach (now in the Grand Duchy of Luxembourg). In another binding, whose main theme is the Crucifixion but *30* whose composition broadens out to include a vast area of theological reflection, the round, youthful faces of the figures place the work in Cologne in about the year 1000.

Although the Western centre of gravity was located in France and Germany, from as early as the time of Charlemagne the empire had some forceful neighbours and rivals to reckon with. One of the most important was the Anglo-Saxon world, where a lively, vivid style based on Carolingian models began to develop, as illustrated in large number of manuscripts. A portable altar is one of the few surviving examples of this trend *28* translated into goldsmith's work. The crushed drapery on the figures of the angels, the Virgin, and Saint John fit in perfectly with the dramatic atmosphere of the Crucifixion. It was this vivacity, either allied with, or in opposition to, Carolingian and Ottonian classicism, which formed the basis of the Romanesque art that was to flourish at the dawn of the new millennium. P.-Y.L.P.

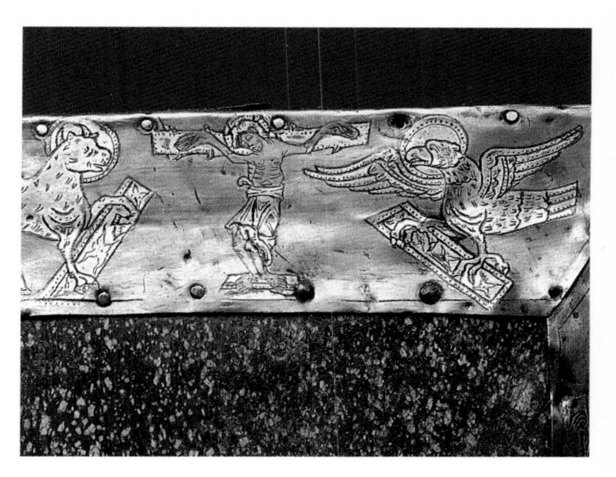

28 Portable altar depicting the Crucifixion (detail)
England, 2nd quarter 11th century
Porphyry, silver gilt, niello

29 Book board depicting the coronation of Otto II and Theophanu
German empire, 982–3
Ivory

30 Book board depicting the Crucifixion
Cologne, *c.* 1000
Ivory

31 Diptych
Obverse: England, 8th century; reverse: northern Italy, *c.* 900
Ivory

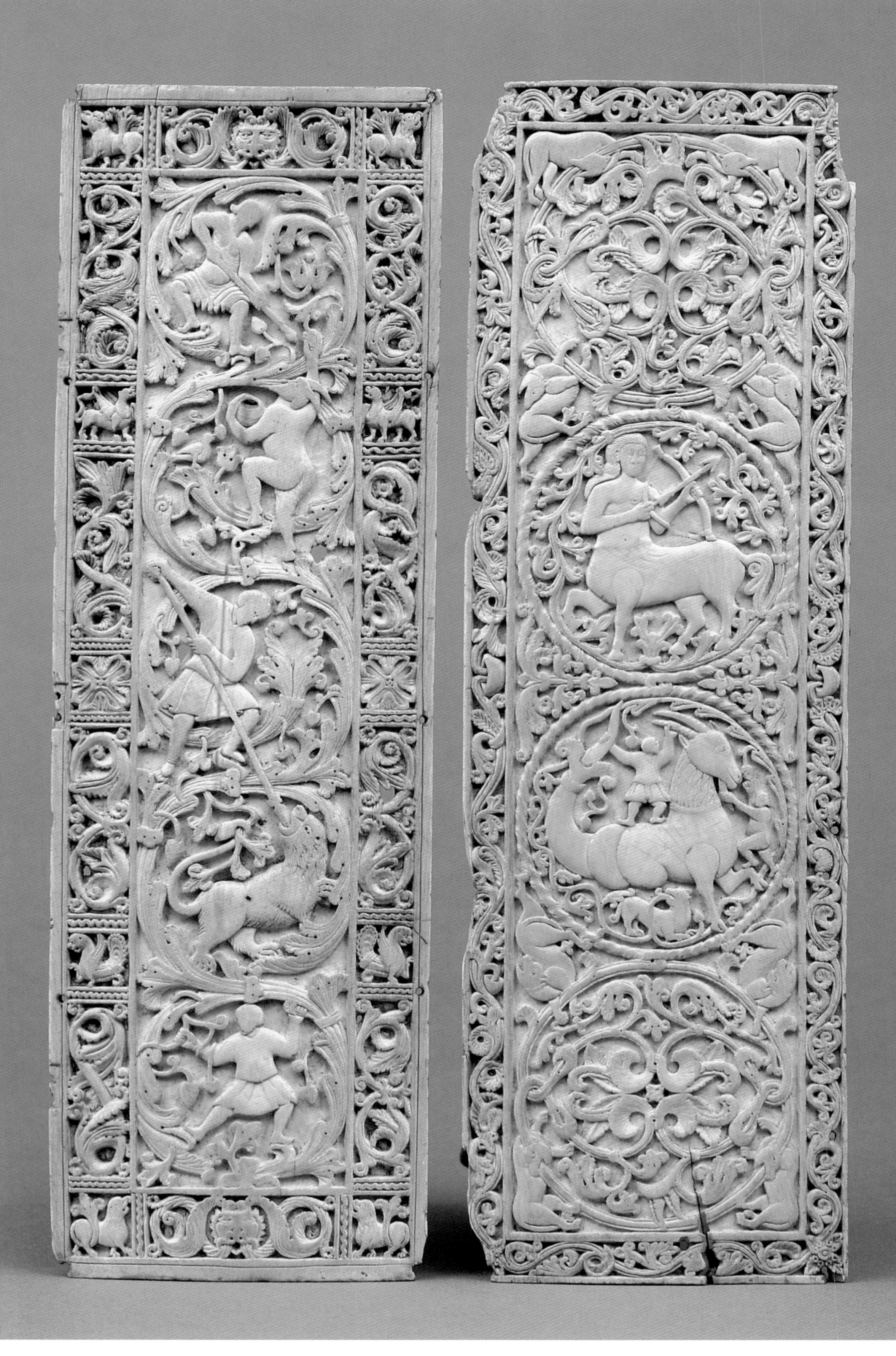

hec est VIA QA DILECTVS DOMIN O BEA ATERBENEDI

Romanesque Art: Paris and Saint-Denis

The period of peace which began in the year 1000 brought with it the blossoming of an original style of art which is termed 'Romanesque' because the societies it embraced, besides having a common feudal system and religious belief, also shared a body of Latin (or Roman) traditions. As the huge architectural programmes of the time indicate, Romanesque art, which was essentially religious in nature, benefited not only from a phase of general expansion in the West, but, more especially, from the meteoric rise of the monastic orders, begun in Cluny, and from the reform of the Church initiated by Gregory VII. By about 1100, Romanesque art had attained a sort of 'classic' balance. The Museum, with its diverse collections, is able to illustrate that period in all its richness and variety, giving pride of place to the art of the Ile-de-France, of which it owns a number of key examples.

One of the most original features of Romanesque art is its habit of drawing on a variety of techniques and traditions deriving from its own locality, from the Carolingian renaissance, and from sources further afield, such as the Byzantine and Islamic world. For this reason, works dating from before 1100 display a particularly high degree of inventiveness. An illuminated initial B from the start of Saint Luke's Gospel, dating from the beginning of the Romanesque period, summarizes this combination of past tradition and nascent innovation. More of a sketch than a painting, with an air of improvisation (spontaneity is one of the essential traits of Romanesque art), the letter is enlivened by a monumental figure of Saint Luke deriving from Carolingian depictions of the Evangelists but used here purely for ornamental purposes. Historiated initials were an Anglo-Norman invention but became popular throughout Europe. The elegant stems and leaves that complete the decoration – a distant borrowing from Byzantium or the Islamic world – are interpreted in a free and vivid style, which, given the presence of the scrolled floral motif, may be ascribed to the monasteries of northern France. It was through these monasteries, occupying, as they did, a key position geographically, that the synthesis between insular and Carolingian art was effected. The same creative ornamental approach is to be found on an ivory head of a bishop's crook (*c.* 1120–30). It is decorated on one side with an eagle and on the other with a lion, each surrounded by scrolls of foliage, and the volute terminates in a dragon's head. The crook has parallels in Anglo-Norman illumination, in precious metalwork (Gloucester candlestick), and in sculpture (Angers, Aulnay, etc.), and it indicates the frequent artistic exchanges that took place between England, Normandy, Anjou, and Aquitaine, which were all linked during the twelfth century, on account of the political situation. An oliphant from the abbey of Saint-Arnoul in Metz illustrates the degree of recycling to which works of art

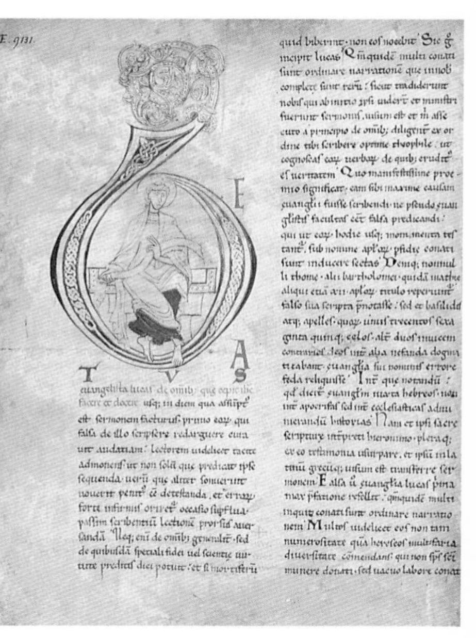

33 Single leaf of manuscript bearing initial B with figure of Saint Luke
Northern France,
2nd half 11th century
Illumination on parchment

32 Monks keeping vigil at the death of Saint Benedict
Saint-Denis, 1140–5
Stained glass

34 Head of a crook
England (?), 1st quarter 12th century
Walrus tusk

35 Oliphant from treasury of Saint-Arnoul abbey, Metz, depicting Christ and the Virgin Enthroned (detail)
Southern Italy, late 11th or early 12th century
Ivory

36 Gospel binding from Novara
Northern Italy (?), early 12th century
Silver, partially gilded, niello decoration, on wooden board, parchment

SCS PETRVS IHESVS CRISTVS SCS PAVLVS

were subject: its decorative frieze actually dates from the Fatimid period and was adapted, in about 1100, by Romanesque artists working under Byzantine influence and here displaying their genius for reuse. A binding for a Gospel book made in Novara (early twelfth century) depicts a *traditio legis*. Byzantium continued to provide Italy with prestigious models, and in the north of the country – in this case, in Novara – these were reinterpreted in a Germanic spirit (note, in particular, the elongated figures and soft lines of the drapery).

Ile-de-France – Centre of Innovation

There was one area in which the Romanesque artist could not but be original, and that was monumental sculpture. Such sculpture was intimately bound up with the buildings whose key features (capitals, portals) it now began to adorn, and it represents Romanesque art's greatest triumph. Its distinctive traits are its subordination to context (figures had to be designed to fit into an architectural framework) and its larger-than-life treatment of form. It spread geographically along with building activity – in other words, across the whole of Europe – and Paris became one of the hubs of innovation. Beginning in about 1050, Saint-Germain-des-Prés, the first abbey to be rebuilt after the invasions, embarked on a very ambitious programme of monumental decoration, for which it drew on a variety of sources, as is shown by the twelve capitals deposited in the Museum. The one depicting a Salvator Mundi, apparently inspired by a Carolingian manuscript or ivory, seems the most original of these, being the most perfected in terms of its attempt to convey volume and monumentality. It is also unique in the subtleness of its iconography, which aims to glorify the Eucharist (Christ is depicted holding a host in his right hand). The abbey would seem here to be affirming its orthodox position at a time when this particular sacrament was the focus of great doctrinal debates. Such a piece indicates the degree to which an iconographical programme was influenced by the sponsor, by the continuing impact of the Carolingian empire on the intellectual élite – particularly as regards providing models – and by the didactic role which the Church assigned to art. The same climate of erudition prevailed in the reconstruction of the abbey of Sainte-Geneviève in about 1100. (One of the teachers at its celebrated school was Peter Abelard, the great champion of the twelfth-century Latin renaissance.) When the church was destroyed in 1807, the Museum salvaged the capitals from four large round piers in the nave; on these is a frieze depicting scenes from the book of Genesis, together with the signs of the Zodiac. The sculptural approach is very different from that in the Saint-Germain capitals, but the subject matter – also treated in Saint-Germain-des-Prés and Saint-Denis – reveals the abbey's great erudition. It also reminds one of Abelard's theories about the Creation, about the division of time, and about the course of the heavenly bodies. Innovative research of this kind would have been unthinkable without royal approval, and it was at about this time that the Capetian dynasty consolidated its power and that the various building programmes began to move forward. Construction work became better organized and more systematic, as is evident from the architects' plans, from the large numbers of workers gathered at the different sites, and from the success in adhering to building schedules. The Ile-de-France was about to embark on a new creative phase.

37 Capital from the nave of Saint-Germain-des-Prés depicting the Salvator Mundi and an Angel
Paris, *c.* 1050
Stone

The royal abbey of Saint-Denis, which began to be built in about 1140, was a magnificent embodiment of the new approaches being tried out at *40* that time. It made use of rib-vaulting to create a different kind of internal space, and, by introducing column statues, it brought a new liveliness to façade design. Whereas Romanesque sculpture had been subordinated to architecture, the column statues of Saint-Denis, and subsequently of *39* Chartres and Notre-Dame de Paris (before 1148), stood free of the walls. *41* It was Abbot Suger, royal adviser (and friend of Louis VI), who had charge of the iconographical programme. The Old Testament, in the shape of the statues of the kings, is figured on elements supporting the

38 Capital from the nave of Sainte-Geneviève, Paris, depicting Zodiacal sign of Gemini
Paris, *c.* 1100
Stone
Deposited by the Ecole des Beaux-Arts

tympana and arching, which, in their turn, feature Christological scenes ranging from the Incarnation to the Redemption. The same subtleness in iconography is found in the stained glass of the choir, completed in 1144. Fascinated by the translucence of the windows and the precious quality of the materials used to make them, Suger and his contemporaries thought of them as an ideal image of the heavenly Jerusalem. The Museum owns the upper part of a stained-glass window depicting the Life of Saint Benedict. Its emphatic style is reminiscent of northern *32* French illumination (Saint-Omer, Saint-Amand), whereas the other stained glass in the abbey, produced by the abbey's main workshop, recalls Mosan traditions, confirming the widespread influence of goldsmith's work from that region. Saint-Denis documents the emergence of a new mode of expression, made possible by the combination of Suger's genius for design and the ability of those cosmopolitan craftsmen whom he summoned to Saint-Denis to translate his ideas into visual form.

From the Meuse to the Limousin

In fact, the birth of Gothic art occurred slightly before Romanesque art had reached its peak in the rest of the kingdom and of Europe. The art that began to blossom in imperial areas such as the valleys of the Meuse and Rhine from the mid-twelfth century was refined, skilful, and much influenced by Antiquity. As well as benefiting from a long artistic tradition, it was carried along by a favourable climate of scholarship. Theologians (such as Rupert of Deutz) helped to create a subtle symbolism based on a typological juxtaposition of episodes from the Old and New Testament. An openwork gilded bronze book-cover depicting the Rivers of Paradise is a superb example of this approach. The rear side depicts *42*

40 Shaft of small column
with rinceaux decoration
Saint-Denis, before 1140
Stone

41 Saint Paul from the Saint Anne portal,
Notre-Dame, Paris, before 1148
Stone

39 Head of a Prophet from the right-
hand portal of the western façade
of Saint-Denis, before 1140
Stone

the Lamb of God and the four rivers of Paradise, identified by a typically Mosan didactic inscription. It was intended to echo a Salvator Mundi surrounded by the four Evangelists which appeared on the front side, now lost. Besides being located in areas where metalworking was highly developed, wealthy abbeys were fortunate in enjoying the support of Wibald, abbot of Stavelot (1130–58), who, as adviser to three German emperors, was able to provide artistic activities with the necessary political impetus. *44* The Museum's retable of the Pentecost marks the high point of Mosan art in Stavelot (or Koblenz) in about 1160–70. Dominated by the bust of Christ, the Apostles are grouped in twos between seven columns representing the Seven Gifts of the Holy Spirit. There is a feeling of real freedom about the figures, and an aura of elegant classicism, and both these traits recall the small statues on the portable altar from Stavelot, or those in the Crucifixion from the abbey of Saint-Bertin in Saint-Omer. The retable's discreet enamelling, meanwhile, echoes that of the reliquary triptych of the True Cross from the Sainte-Croix church in Liège.

42 Book board depicting
the Rivers of Paradise
Mosan, mid-12th century
Gilded copper

43 Reliquary plaque depicting
the Crucifixion
Hildesheim (Lower Saxony), *c.* 1170
Copper, *champlevé* enamel, gilding

In Saxony, another great centre of art, the classical influence was less marked, and there was less emphasis on symbolism, despite the fact that imperial art was used as a model by the rival dynasty of the Guelphs. An example is provided by a small plaque depicting the crucified Christ between *43* the Church and the Synagogue (*c.* 1170), the pendant to which is now in Brussels. The gilded figures stand out against an enamelled background in cool, muted tones. From Lower Saxony, which was known more for its bronze liturgical implements, we also have an altar-frontal *49* from the monastery of Huysburg, near Halberstadt (1150–60). Although its iconography (Apostles surrounding an enthroned Christ) is traditional for Romanesque pieces of this kind, the fact that it has survived, and the materials from which it is made – silk and linen – make it a very special item. In contrast to Rhenish-Mosan goldsmith's work, which was intended for a handful of connoisseurs and wealthy individuals, the enamelwork of the south introduces us to a special kind of production designed for widespread distribution. Serially produced 'Limoges' enamels were made in secular workshops, though their success would have been unthinkable without the support of the powerful Cluniac abbey of Saint-Martial in

44 Retable of the Pentecost (detail)
Mosan, 13th century
Copper, *champlevé* enamel, gilding

DE·C·EALO·SONVS

Limoges. The abbey was the main purchaser and distributor of this type of enamel, and its sumptuous library provided many designs for it. In great contrast to Mosan or Parisian art, the Limoges work was not produced at the behest of someone close to the emperor or king – although it did later enjoy the patronage of the Plantagenets; nor did it draw on a theological, moral, or dialectical repertoire determined by noted clerics. Its prime purpose was to satisfy a local demand (and later the requirements of the Benedictine order) for liturgical objects such as shrines and reliquaries (veneration of relics was becoming extremely popular at this

45 Historiated shrine
of Saint Thomas Becket
Limoges, late 12th century
Copper, *champlevé* enamel, gilding

time), censers, candlesticks, processional crosses, bindings, and so on. And it was the lives of saints from the region, or to whom the region was particularly devoted, which determined its iconography. The latter was of a narrative and lively, though ultimately repetitive, style. The only examples in the Museum are the small shrines dedicated to Saint Thomas Becket. Limoges enamelwork experienced a meteoric rise in about 1160 but continued to prosper over two centuries, making its way to every corner of Europe. A binding depicting the Salvator Mundi poses the delicate and as yet unresolved problem of the appearance of *champlevé* enamel in places other than Limoges. (This local *champlevé* technique is also to be seen in the Reliquary of Saint Henry in the Louvre.) Recalling as it does the 'Urna', that major work of art of Santo Domingo de Silos (now in Burgos), the binding (which has a counterpart in a collection in Madrid) may well be of Spanish origin. It is admirable for the delicacy and range of its colours, the unassuming proportions of the attached head, and the evanescent quality of the figure of Christ. Various workshops in central and south-western France and the north of Spain seem to have engaged in the same kind of workmanship as Limoges, but the task of identifying them remains a complex one. Sometimes Limoges work was used for individual commissions, resulting in the creation of some exceptional pieces. The abbey at Grandmont, for example, was a prestigious patron of Limoges production. In about 1189, it commissioned a high altar in honour of Etienne de Muret, the founder of the order at Grandmont, who had died in 1124 and had recently been canonized. The two large panels in the Museum are the only parts of this major decorative ensemble – depicting scenes from the Life of Christ

46 Panel from main altar
of the church of Grandmont
depicting the Adoration of the Magi
Limoges, *c.* 1190
Copper, *champlevé* enamel, gilding

47 Book binding depicting
the Salvator Mundi
Limousin region or Spain,
3rd quarter 12th century
Copper, *champlevé* enamel, gilding

and the lives of the saints – to have survived. They capture Limoges enamel at its peak: the figure of the Infant Christ being presented to the Magi is gilded and carved, and its head is in *mezzo relievo*, whereas the other figures and motifs are still only picked out in colour. The palette is a lively but subtly graduated one (note especially the rosy hue of the flesh). The whole work, very refined in its execution, achieves a sort of classical balance. Because it was created in 1189, the altar does not yet reflect the naturalist tendencies that were in vogue north of the Loire. Another traditional type of production in the Middle Ages, on a par with that of enamels and depictions of the Virgin and Child, is represented by the monumental Crucifixion from Le Puy. It reflects the advent of an increasingly sentimental style of devotion. *46* *48*

Heralds of Change

A similar spirit pervades a group of Catalan capitals resembling those in Gerona cathedral. They were originally to be found in a cloister – a favourite location for Romanesque sculpture – and they depict various episodes from the book of Genesis. The most striking one shows Abraham bowing low before three angels to whom he offers hospitality, and who will later reveal themselves to be the messengers of Yahveh. Despite their squat stature, the figures, clothed in long, flowing *draperie mouillée* and pictured in very gentle attitudes, are typical of the great classicizing movement which began in Italy and spread through all the regions bordering the Mediterranean in the late twelfth and early thirteenth century. The same classicizing legacy is discernible in fragments of a mural from the abbey of Charlieu (Loire), whose huge enthroned Christ, now lost, recalled that, also lost, of the porch in Vézelay, or of the refectory in Lavaudieu (Haute-Loire). *51* *50*

In a period when classical literature was exercising great fascination, artists in southern Europe were greatly influenced by classicizing and Byzantine trends. In an attempt to achieve realism and individualization, they began to depict the human figure in soft draperies and comparatively relaxed attitudes. The artist who best illustrates this *style 1200* is the Mosan goldsmith Nicolas de Verdun, but illuminators and glass-painters from Soissons, Laon, and Champagne, who were in contact with Mosan art, also proved highly inventive. The Museum owns one of the stained-glass panels from the now-dispersed set of windows from the cathedral in Troyes. The panel is notable for the elegance and authority of its figures, their elongated but harmonious proportions, the serried pleats of their drapery, and their classical-style heads. The medallion window depicting the Resurrection of the Dead, discovered in the Sainte-Chapelle and deposited with the Museum, testifies, as does Saint-Denis before it, to the continuing influence of the North in Paris. (The use of rinceaux in the background recalls Mosan enamelwork.) Paris, capital of the kingdom of France, seat of the royal family, and a city in the full throes of expansion, did adopt the *style 1200* for a while; but signs of renewed stylistic change came as early as 1210–20, in the sculptural decoration of the portal commemorating the Coronation of the Virgin in Notre-Dame. From then on, Paris was to become the centre from which Gothic art would establish its influence. *53* *52*

S.L.

49 Altar-frontal from Huysburg
Germany (Lower Saxony),
c. 1150–60
Embroidery in linen and silk

50 Head of an Apostle
Charlieu, refectory of the abbey
Burgundy, *c.* 1200
Mural painting

48 *Crucifixion* (detail)
Auvergne, 12th century
Polychrome painting on wood

52 *Resurrection of the Dead*
Paris, Sainte-Chapelle, *c.* 1200
Stained glass

53 *The Charity of Saint Nicholas*
Troyes, cathedral of Saint-Pierre, late 12th century
Stained glass

51 Cloister capital depicting the three angels being welcomed by Abraham
Catalonia, late 12th century
Stone

Western Sculpture from the Thirteenth to the Early Sixteenth Century

Monumental Sculpture in Paris

It was the construction sites of the great cathedrals of northern France which provided the impetus for the development of monumental sculpture in the thirteenth century. The latter is particularly well represented in the Museum, thanks to the many fragments that have come to it from the neighbouring cathedral of Notre-Dame de Paris.

A room has been specially created to display the Notre-Dame pieces, *56* which came to light in a series of discoveries between 1839 and 1977. The display enables the visitor to take in, at a glance, more than a century of Parisian sculpture, documenting formal changes across that period.

Along with the reinstated Saint Anne portal, two other portals were *41* added to the western façade of the building between 1210 and 1220. The central one, devoted to the theme of the Resurrection, was damaged even before the Revolution, when, in 1771, Soufflot, at the request of the Notre-Dame chapter, undertook to have access at this point widened. The trumeau was removed and the two lintels were carved into an arcade shape. When Viollet-le-Duc carried out his restoration of the cathedral, he removed parts of the lintels, and these were given to the Museum. On the fragments from the lower lintel, angels are sounding their *55* trumpets as the dead emerge from their graves. A marked difference in style between the right and left parts of the scene would seem to indicate that the left-hand side is of later date.

But the most spectacular set of sculptures in this room is the group of heads from the Kings' Gallery on the façade of Notre-Dame, discovered *57* by chance in 1977 in Rue de la Chaussée d'Antin in Paris. The statues of the kings of Judah, Christ's forebears, which had traditionally long been held to represent the kings of France, were destroyed during the Terror: their severed heads were auctioned off and bought up by one of the brothers of Lakanal, the famous regicide member of the National Convention. Unlike his brother, this Lakanal was a royalist, and he had the heads carefully buried in the courtyard of the private mansion which he was then having built for himself. Having lain buried and forgotten for almost two centuries, they were discovered when works were carried out on the building, which has since become the headquarters of the Banque Française du Commerce Extérieur. The bank donated them to the Museum. Although they suffered considerable damage at the hands of the revolutionary vandals, the twenty-one heads have retained traces of their colouring – a rare example of original cathedral decoration. The colours were extremely bright – yellow, dark blue or black for the hair, red for the cheeks and lips, black or green for the eyes – and the painting is extremely finely done. The decoration gives the kings an air of intensity and accentuates the subtle modelling.

The sculpture from the northern and southern sides of the building, and

54 *Adam* from Notre-Dame, Paris
Paris, *c.* 1260
Stone

55 Fragments of lower lintel depicting the Resurrection of the Dead from central portal of western façade, Notre-Dame, Paris, *c.* 1210–20
Stone

56 View of the Notre-Dame of Paris room
Paris, Notre-Dame, *c.* 1220–30
Stone

57 Head of King Judah from Notre-Dame, Paris
Paris, *c.* 1220–30
Polychrome painting on stone

from the portals at either end of the transept, document the developments that took place in sculpture in the second half of the thirteenth century. A figure of Adam that was part of Notre-Dame's interior decoration is a masterpiece of Gothic sculpture, in which life-size nudes such as this are rare. A matching statue of Eve is now lost. Adam is depicted after the Fall, and his features are suffused with a melancholy sensuality.

54

A considerable influence was to be exerted on Gothic art by another great Parisian building lodge – that of the Sainte-Chapelle, built between 1243 and 1248 to house the relics of the Passion procured by Saint Louis. Besides the dazzling stained-glass windows, which literally form a wall of glass, the decoration of the Sainte-Chapelle included a series of sculptures. In the upper chapel, figures of the twelve Apostles were placed in front of the pillars, thus symbolizing the 'pillars of the Church'. All of them were removed during the Revolution, but six were not restored to their original positions during the nineteenth century and made their way into the Museum's collection. The figures – particularly that of the Apostle known as *le mélancolique* – reveal the classical bent of Parisian art in the mid-thirteenth century. The serenity and gravity of the features, the soberness of the bearing and drapery – the figure's whole expression tends towards balance and harmony.

60

The *style rayonnant* exemplified in the Sainte-Chapelle had an enduring effect on late thirteenth-century architecture. Evidence of this may be seen in the portal of the Chapel of the Virgin built in the abbey of Saint-Germain-des-Prés by the architect Pierre de Montreuil, who also designed the southern section of the Notre-Dame transept and parts of the abbey of Saint-Denis.

58

The head of the recumbent statue of Jeanne de Toulouse, wife of Alphonse de Poitiers, Saint Louis's brother, is also of Parisian origin. Jeanne de Toulouse died in 1271 and was buried in the abbey at Gercy which she and her husband had founded. The execution of her statue was evidently entrusted to one of the finest Parisian craftsmen of the second half of the thirteenth century, as is clear from the great simplicity and purity of the features.

59

Courtly demand and royal commissions continued to shape artistic production at the end of the thirteenth century. One of the great creations of the time of Philippe le Bel, for example, was the programme of sculpture for the church of Saint-Louis in Poissy, a Dominican priory which the king founded at the place where his grandfather Louis IX had been born, following the latter's canonization in 1297.

The iconography was intended to glorify the king's devout ancestor, and with him the whole Capetian dynasty. Besides depictions of the royal family – Saint Louis, Marguerite de Provence, and six of their children (only two of these figures are known to have survived, namely that of Pierre d'Alençon, which is now in the Museum, and that of Isabelle de France, now in Notre-Dame in Poissy) – the series comprised a Passion cycle, from which several angels have survived. The site of the former abbey, which was destroyed in the Revolution, belonged to the painter Meissonier, who made a gift of various fragments of the sculptural decoration to his friend the sculptor Geoffroy-Dechaume. It was through the family of the latter, a friend and colleague of Viollet-le-Duc, that a number of the Poissy angels made their way into the Museum's collection. Depicted carrying various instruments of the Passion or sounding trumpets at the Last Judgement, the angels mark a stylistic turning-point, heralding developments that were to take place in the fourteenth cen-

58 Pierre de Montreuil
Portal of Chapel of the Virgin
Paris, Saint-Germain-des-Prés, 1245
Stone

59 Head of the recumbent statue of Jeanne de Toulouse
Paris region, after 1271
Stone

60 *Apostle* from the Sainte-Chapelle,
Paris, 1241–8
Stone

61 *Angel* from the collegiate
church in Poissy
Ile-de-France, after 1297
Stone

62 Robert de Lannoy
Saint James
Paris, between 1319 and 1324

63 *Presentation in the Temple*
Paris, *c.* 1370–80
Stone

64 *Virgin and Child* from the abbey at Longchamp
Paris, mid-14th century
Marble

tury, namely a trend to more fluid and supple drapery and an apparent simplicity of form. *61*

A particularly good example of this early fourteenth-century style is afforded by the figures of the Apostles which adorned the hostel of Saint-Jacques-aux-Pèlerins, founded by the royal family and the burghers of Paris to accommodate pilgrims to Santiago de Compostela. Thanks to the hostel's accounts, we know the names of the sculptors who produced this group of Apostles, of which only five are known to have survived. Two were made by Guillaume de Nourriche between 1319 and 1324, and the rest of the group – notably Saint James, recognizable by his shell-adorned scrip – were carved by Robert de Lannoy between 1319 and 1327. *62*

Although a few of the individual artists' names begin to emerge from the fourteenth century onwards, thanks to written sources, especially accounts and inventories, it is not always possible to say which of the items that have come down to us are a particular sculptor's work. Conversely, many masterpieces of the time cannot be attributed to any particular artist. A very fine marble relief of the Presentation in the Temple, for example, has been attributed both to André Beauneveu and to Jean de Liège, two of the artists who dominated Parisian artistic production in the last quarter of the fourteenth century. *63*

The great Virgin and Child from the abbey at Longchamp, dating from the same period, remains unascribed. Sculpted in marble and heightened with a few traces of gold, it summarizes the trend in sculpture at the end of the fourteenth century, which sought to create a highly refined impression by a subtle and deliberately simple use of materials. The theme of the Virgin and Child, one of the most frequently depicted in the fourteenth century, offers huge scope for the expression of the relationship between the Infant Jesus and his mother, involving a range of emotions from laughter, through tenderness, to melancholy, and so on. *64*

65 *Virgin and Child* (detail)
Dijon, 2nd quarter
15th century
Stone

Burgundian Sculpture

The medieval image-maker's art underwent a radical renewal at the beginning of the fifteenth century, under the influence of the sculptors brought together at the court of the Duke of Burgundy. Claus Sluter, appointed by the duke to provide the decoration for the charterhouse at Champmol, the burial place of the dukes of Burgundy, abandoned the refined elegance of fourteenth-century sculpture in favour of expressive power. Few of his works survive, but his personality had a lasting effect on the artists of the fifteenth century.

Several of the sculptures in the Museum perfectly illustrate the Burgundian style established by Sluter. The Virgin and Child known as the Virgin of the Petition, is a fine example, with its heavily slanted hips and densely pleated cloak echoing the skilful drapery of the Flemish primitives. The ample contours of the cloak contrast with the tiny face that emerges from it, a finely featured, youthful face tinged with sadness as it contemplates the Child. This is no surprise, since Burgundian sculpture sought deliberately to convey emotions with great intensity through the use of expressive drapery and realistic features. Similar features may be seen on a statue of Saint James as a Pilgrim, with its jutting cheekbones and deep furrows (see ill. page 2). A small devotional retable depicting the Lamentation is part of the same trend. It ranks amongst the finest creations of Burgundian art, and was perhaps produced by the circle of Claus de Werve, nephew of, and successor to, Sluter. *65* *67*

66 The Virgin and Saint John
Tuscany, early 13th century
Polychrome painting on wood

Although particularly rich in French sculpture, the Museum's collection also offers a variety of insights into the development of this major medieval art in the other countries of Europe.

Italy

In Italy, monumental sculpture experienced a revival in about 1200, under the influence of the great French construction sites, notably that of Chartres. It is from this early thirteenth-century period that two exceptional figures of the Virgin and Saint John date, originally part of a Deposition. *66* This theme was rarely depicted in the West before the ninth century but became particularly popular in Catalonia and Italy in the transition from the twelfth to the thirteenth century: more than twenty such groups, executed in coloured wood, date from this period. The figure of Saint John provides both a counterpart and a contrast to that of the Virgin, in an arrangement that juxtaposes the soft, continuous lines of the Virgin's drapery with the sharper, more abrupt contours of that of Saint John. The grief is focused in Saint John's face; as with the Virgin, his whole demeanour constitutes an appeal to the Christian to become involved in the drama of the Passion and to share in Christ's sufferings.

67 *Lamentation*
Burgundy, 1st half 15th century
Polychrome painting on wood

The popularity of this theme in thirteenth-century Italy was associated with the emergence of Franciscan devotion which aimed to make Christ's humanity tangible and bring him closer to the faithful.

Equally imposing, though this time in an unmistakably earthly domain, 68 is a statue of a doctor of the University of Bologna. Bologna was one of the oldest and most prestigious of the universities of Europe, being particularly noted for its legal studies. Its doctors were therefore high-ranking individuals, as is clear from their marble tombs, on which they are depicted exercising their scholarly functions. This doctor adopts a hieratic pose, seated in his professor's chair and fixing his audience with a majestic and authoritative gaze. Death does not seem to have interrupted his learned discourse.

68 *Doctor of the University discoursing*
Bologna, *c.* 1340
Marble

As elsewhere in the Western world, churches in Italy in the fourteenth century were adorned with statues of the saints. Central Italy, particularly Tuscany, had a fondness for subtly coloured wooden carvings. The monumental figures may sometimes appear in groups, as is the case in an Annunciation; or they may stand alone, as does that of a Sienese Saint John the Baptist of elongated proportions, with emaciated features and clothed in a red cloak. In contrast, another piece of sculpture from Siena, the reli- 69 quary bust of Saint Mabille, one of Saint Ursula's companions, presents us with a serene image of a martyr calmly contemplating her fate.

Northern Sculpture

Whereas in Italy retables were a favoured domain of painters, German altarpieces often combined painting and sculpture. The closing centuries of the Middle Ages were a truly golden age in the field of retable carving. The favourite material for German artists was the soft wood of the lime-tree, which allowed elaborate designs and gave the artist an opportunity 70 to display all his virtuosity. This is the case in a statue of Saint Christopher, one of the most popular saints at the close of the Middle Ages, because he was reputed to protect one from sudden death.

The light-coloured wood of the lime-tree was rarely left in its original state, and the sculptor's work was generally complemented by skilful 71 polychrome painting. In a Virgin and Child group, for example, the colours have iconographical significance and thus determine the work's meaning. Closed, it looks like a straightforward enthroned Virgin and Child; but in its open state, it acquires added meaning: at the centre is a Trinity, with God the Father holding the crucified Christ (the crucifix is modern, and the dove representing the Holy Spirit has been lost); the inner faces of the painted wings, meanwhile, depict particular individuals placed under the protection of the Virgin of Mercy.

German retables were often made up of a combination of sculpture in the central section and painting on the shutters. A perfect example of a private devotional version of the genre is a retable attributed to Master 72 Arnt of Kalkar (Lower Rhine). On the outer sides of the wings are a Nativity and an Adoration of the Magi; on the inner sides, six small panels depict the various stages of the Passion. In the centre, the sculpted part offers a dramatic representation of the Lamentation: the Virgin, Saint John, and the holy women busy themselves around the stiffened body of Christ, whilst the donor, a Carthusian monk, under the guidance of Saint Andrew, kneels in prayer before Christ. The very fine polychromy, which is exceptionally well preserved, enhances the quivering sensitivity of the sculptures. The scene of Christ in the Garden of Olives depicted

70 *Saint Christopher*
Southern Germany, *c.* 1500
Lime

69 Angelo di Nalduccio (?)
Reliquary bust of Saint Mabille
Siena, *c.* 1370–80
Polychrome painting on wood

71 *Virgin and Child Enthroned*
West Prussia, *c.* 1400
Polychrome painting on lime

72 Master Arnt
Passion retable from Kranenburg
Kalkar (Lower Rhineland), *c.* 1483
Polychrome painting on wood
and painted wings

on the left-hand wing is a common one in medieval iconography. It was popularized through engravings and was then translated into painting and sculpture – in both wood and stone. It appears in a fragment of a large retable attributed to the workshop of the Fribourg sculptor Hans Geiler. A single item from this – a figure of Christ at prayer – entered the Museum's collections in 1903. Much later, in 1993, a fragment that was clearly from the same source – the Apostles sleeping on the Mount of Olives – appeared on the art market, and it was thus possible to complete the scene. *74*

The growing importance of images in devotional life at the end of the Middle Ages explains the increased production of the retable in all its forms, and also, in particular, the development of specialized, standardized retable production in certain artistic centres. This was the case in England in the fifteenth century, in the area around Nottingham, where there were alabaster quarries. The alabaster was worked into small panels depicting individual scenes – the Annunciation, episodes from the Passion, the Resurrection – which could then be assembled according to the iconography and size of retable required. The altarpieces – often rudimentary in style, but very popular, since they were exported all over Europe – were then finished off with a very bright polychrome decoration. *73*

A quasi-industrial approach also characterized Brabantine retable production in the early sixteenth century, particularly in Antwerp. The Museum owns two examples in polychrome wood: a Passion altarpiece and the Averbode retable, both of which have lost their painted wings. The closely guarded quality of Antwerp retables was guaranteed by the severed-hand hallmark of the Guild of Saint Luke – an allusion to the legend of the foundation of Antwerp, according to which a giant used to take sailors to ransom and then cut their hands off and throw them into the river Scheldt. Retables of this kind enjoyed international popularity because of their low cost and simple iconographical content: they were veritable 'Bibles for the illiterate', illustrating mainly scenes from the Passion and the Childhood of Christ. This very simple representation of the basic Christian message is rounded off with architectural niches containing small scenes depicting the seven sacraments. The outstanding feature of the Passion scenes is their narrative character: they are peopled by a seething mass of figures with dramatic facial expressions. In the Carrying of the Cross, the women's outlandish hairstyles, the rich brocade of their clothes, the intricate and unusual weaponry, and a number of delectable details such as the child with its wooden horse, cannot have failed to attract the eye of the faithful, evoking the atmosphere of mystery plays. *75*

The same mood, combining religious theme with secular treatment, pervades a Brabantine statue of Mary Magdalene. The saint's elegant bearing and elaborate hairstyle do more to catch the eye of the believer than does the jar of ointment recalling the body of the crucified Christ. The trend towards an extremely worldly depiction of the saints is clearly visible in a figure of Saint Barbara of the same period. It was against this type of representation of the saints, which brought them far too close to the faithful, and against the resultant over-secularization of their cult, that the Protestant Reformation was soon to react. *76* *77*

E.A.

74 Workshop of Hans Geiler
Sleeping Apostles on the Mount of Olives
Fribourg (Switzerland), *c.* 1520–5
Polychrome painting on lime

73 *Resurrection*
Nottingham, 15th century
Polychrome painting on alabaster

75 Passion retable
Antwerp, 1st quarter 16th century
Polychrome painting on wood

76 *Mary Magdalene*
Brussels, end 15th century
Oak

77 *Saint Barbara*
Normandy (?), late 15th century
Stone

Painting, Illumination, and Stained Glass from the Thirteenth to the Sixteenth Century

The new Gothic style made its way more belatedly into painting than into architecture. The change only began in the second quarter of the thirteenth century. It coincided with a new political situation in the Western world, in which two powers – the Capetian and Plantagenet monarchies – were ranged against a dismembered Empire. The French royal domain, that is to say the Ile-de-France, was the centre from which the new art, a symbol of the kingdom's greatness, began its spread. Its influence was first felt in the towns, which were then undergoing rapid development and had become centres of secular culture. In painting, its chief characteristic was a slow but steady shift towards realism.
During the thirteenth century, Paris, the capital of the kingdom, benefited from the presence not only of the monarchs and the court, but also of a young and prestigious university. Interest in secular literature, the study of Roman law, and the teaching of dialectics fostered the emergence of an intellectual élite and the development of scholasticism. The art of disputation requires an ability to express thought in a clear and logical way, and books soon began to reflect this new requirement in tangible form, as illustrated in an illuminated leaf from a legal manuscript preserved in the Museum: the page is clearly arranged, divided into paragraphs, and marked off with coloured initials. The text, in closely serried script (an attempt to save on parchment) has a marginal commentary or gloss. The preoccupation with order and readability which influenced architecture and pervaded the world of books also affected sculpture and, subsequently, painting, where a new conception of man and reality began to manifest itself. By about 1200, the beginnings of this change had produced a fluid, classicizing style, which then gave way to a more truly Gothic response, of a more energetic and systematic kind.

79

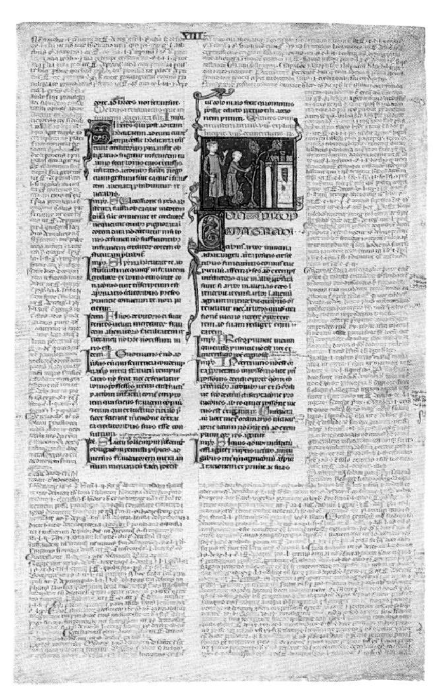

79 Page from a legal manuscript depicting tree-pruning
Paris, 2nd half 13th century
Illumination on parchment

A New Definition of Painting

During the thirteenth century, the dominant art-form was stained glass. The architectural trend towards larger windows offered it unprecedented scope for development, leading to the eclipse of great mural painting, and its power was such that it managed also to supplant illumination, which clung to the *style 1200* and, in an attempt to re-create the very special effects of light, went as far as to adopt gold backgrounds. The panels from the abbey of Gercy (Seine-et-Marne) convey a new mood. The windows illustrating the Life of Saint Martin were made in about 1220, and the scene illustrating the miracle of the pine-tree, in which the bishop saint is seen diverting a pine-tree about to fall on three pagans, is extremely coherent in its composition. The attitudes and ges-

80

78 Antependium. Detail showing the Nativity
Suffolk, England, *c.* 1335
Panel painting

tures of the figures are highly readable, and the figures themselves stand out clearly against a discreetly decorated background in muted colours. Stained glass thus helped define the new style of painting.

81 The Sainte-Chapelle, designed as a huge translucent shrine to house the precious relics of the Passion, endorsed the new style, enhancing it with a typically Parisian refinement and exceptional proportions. The glazed

80 *The Miracle of the Pine-Tree*
Varennes-Gercy, abbey of Gercy (Seine-et-Oise), *c.* 1230
Stained glass

81 Sacrificial scene
Paris, Sainte-Chapelle, 1243–8
Stained glass

area is huge. The lancet windows, narrow but very tall, feature a series of medallions set one above the other. As in the case of the portal sculptures of the same date, there is a global iconographic scheme, beginning in this case with Genesis and ending with the Day of Judgement. The biblical cycle is complemented by a History of the Translation of the Relics. The unified style reminds one that this was a royal commission, completed in a very short space of time, probably under the direction of a single master. Surrounded by medallions of various shapes, each scene is enclosed in an architectural framework in a design that also occurs repeatedly in manuscript illumination of the period (see, for example, the Maciejowski Bible in the Pierpont Morgan Library, or the Paris Psalter or Psalter of Saint Louis in the Bibliothèque Nationale in Paris). The compositions are airy, the range of colours pure, the draughtsmanship firm and unhesitating. The figures are depicted in elegant poses, the lines of the drapery are untrammelled and fluid. The relative bareness of the borders is offset by the decoration of the mosaic-like background, chequered with heraldic motifs. The windows perfectly embody the ambiguous status which stained glass occupies between monumental and decorative art. Its spiritual message has acquired a moral undertone, reflecting the scholastic influence of the day. But the greatest innovation is the truly political dimension conferred on it: by emphasizing the sacredness of the person of the king, it indicates a new political resolve to extol not just the institution of royalty, but the king himself, as successor to the kings of the Old Testament.

Courtly Refinement and the Quest for Realism

King Louis IX, a great patron of the arts and a keen collector of illuminated manuscripts, built up a sumptuous library. However, the presence of the university also prompted a considerable increase in book production and led to the creation of the earliest secular workshops illuminating books for a larger public. Miniature painting began to free itself from the allure of stained glass and established itself as the dominant art-form. Courtly refinement, the presence of architectural elements, and the attempt to achieve three-dimensionality are the typical features of painting at this time, as it hesitates between a predilection for line and a quest for realism.

There was a very early trend towards greater clarity in stained glass. The Apostle windows from Rouen (originally from the château?) are composed of areas of clear *grisaille* with plant motifs, contrasting with continuous figured bands in colour in the centre. In a trend common to both illumination and architecture in Normandy (Fécamp, Rouen, Evreux, etc.), the draughtsmanship becomes less monumental and more mannered. This tendency probably reflected developments in Paris, and it took a different form in the eastern part of France. The range of colours there continued to be very bright, with blues and reds predominating, both in the chequered background and in the large areas of *grisaille*. (An example is the windows of the Franciscan convent in Colmar, dating from the early fourteenth century.)

82

82 *Saint Paul*
Rouen, *c.* 1270
Stained glass

The discovery, in about 1300, of a new stain – silver yellow – that could either be applied on top of other colours in the body of the glass or used on its own freed the glass-painter of the need to cut the glass into small pieces. The resultant reduction in the amount of leading, together with other technical innovations (for example, the production of a 'whiter' form of glass), brought considerable changes to the overall appearance of stained glass. A small panel of decorative *grisaille* heightened with silver yellow and bearing a small clasp-like motif at the centre has recently been identified as coming from the abbey of Saint-Denis (from the Saint-Louis chapel, built in about 1324). It is the earliest of a set of very transparent windows of the fourteenth and fifteenth centuries. The same quest for extreme refinement and courtly elegance, combined with an experimental approach to shade and volume, led Jean Pucelle, the king's painter, to make use of grisaille in his *Hours of Jeanne d'Evreux* (1325–8). Besides affecting book illumination this fashion also extended to painting on fabric (cf. the Sainte-Chapelle mitre, *c.*1350–70) and to sculpture (cf. the use of marble or alabaster with minimum heightening in gold). Parisian enamelwork, meanwhile, was engaged in a similar quest for translucence.

But the use of colour did not disappear entirely from French painting, which, from the beginning of the fourteenth century, began to be affected by the great changes in Italian art. Pucelle was the first French painter to incorporate the Italian innovations in respect of volume, architecture, and the human body. Outside Paris, assimilation was slower. A Crucifixion panel painted in Auvergne in the second quarter of the century does not yet convey any sense of depth. Nor does an English 78 altar-frontal depicting the Life of the Virgin. Probably made for the Dominican priory in Thetford, Suffolk, the altar-frontal is exceptional for its rarity, for its size, and also for its background motifs in relief. (An altarpiece decorated with figures of the saints, attributed to the same artist, is also preserved in Suffolk.) Its iconography and style remind us that the mendicant orders favoured a gentler, Marian spirituality, and that, having abandoned their early poverty, they went on to prove their unerring good taste in the matter of artistic commissions. The graceful bearing of the figures in the panel is reminiscent of Parisian works, which continued to exercise considerable fascination.

83 Page from a breviary belonging to Gérard de Montaigu depicting the Crucifixion
Paris, *c.* 1415–20
Illumination on parchment

From International Gothic to the Conquest of Reality

It was from Paris, in about 1400, that various new refined and courtly tendencies were to emerge and spread rapidly to the whole of Europe – hence the term 'International Gothic'. This was the style of the princely courts, of Charles VI and his uncles, the dukes of Anjou, Berry, and Burgundy, who were great patrons of the arts and lavish collectors. From here it spread to all the other courts of Europe. Confronted with the misfortunes of the time, all these nobles seem to have wanted to escape into an ideal world of chivalry, a world of dreams and aesthetic charm that was to come to an abrupt end with the assassination of Jean sans Peur at Montereau (1419). This interlude of 'Gothic folly' proved extremely fertile. Since most of the painted panels of the time have disappeared, illuminated manuscripts here provide us with invaluable evidence – which is entirely appropriate, given the predilection of princes for illuminated books (see, for example, the *Très Riches Heures du duc de Berry*). Given the similar tastes of the individuals commissioning the works of art, and given the constant toing and froing of both clients and artists, it is natural that International Gothic should display a high degree of stylistic unity. 83 A small Crucifixion from the breviary of Gérard de Montaigu (bishop of Paris from 1410 to 1420) belongs to this trend. With its abstract chequerboard background, already an established device in the fourteenth century, this page evidently owes much to previous artistic currents; but, following in the footsteps of Pucelle, the drawing, the fluidity of the figures, and the overall elegance bear the stamp of Siena. In addition, with its gentle tones and great refinement it has the appeal of a jewel and must have satisfied the aesthetic expectations of an aristocratic clientele.

But the Renaissance had already begun to take hold in Italy. The Low Countries, great economic powers, had entered their artistic golden age. In the other European states, notably France, which was then ravaged by war (civil and foreign), the last embers of Gothic were glowing. The style known as Flamboyant or Late Gothic conveys a feeling of excess and anxiety, but it also mirrors greater social amalgamation. In painting, various foreign influences sanction the reappearance of realism.

Developments in architecture brought a trend towards the creation of wide bays with tall lancets filled with stained glass. It was only in about

84 *Resurrection*
Church of Betton (Ille-et-Vilaine), early 15th century
Stained glass

85 Chess players
Villefranche-sur-Saône, Hôtel de la Bessée, 1430–40
Stained glass

1420 that the east-end windows of churches in Brittany, traditionally devoted to the various episodes of the Passion story, began to break away from a medallion-style layout. The church in Betton (Ille-et-Vilaine) illustrates the new – and very late – arrangement, in which scenes are set under architectural canopies and use is made of white glass heightened with silver yellow. It is one of the very last manifestations of International Gothic. The combination of *grisaille* and silver yellow in a secular panel depicting chess-players is explained by the fact that it was made for a private house at Villefranche-sur-Saône, and for a clientele of aristocratic rank. The subject matter, inspired by the literature of the time (perhaps *Les Echecs amoureux*) shows the degree to which secular themes had made their way into painting.

The work of the glass-painter Peter Hemmel of Andlau, which was to be found all over the eastern part of France and even some way into Germany, was confined mainly to churches. Typical of a kind of serial production that flourished at the end of the Middle Ages, his windows frequently drew their inspiration from German engravings (Master E.S., Schongauer, and so on). The figures, representing either donors or saints (the object of many an entreaty in the late Middle Ages) are pictured against damask-like blue or red backgrounds, under architectural canopies of branches and flowers. Some of the details (hands, armour) are of an elegant refinement typical of the late fifteenth century. In the example shown here, the figure of the knight-cum-donor from the Fleckenstein family, portrayed in realistic fashion, assumes a new kind of monumentality.

86 *The Jouvenel des Ursins Family* (detail)
Paris, *c.* 1445–9
Panel painting

Because of the depredations it suffered, not much is known of fifteenth-century Parisian painting, and the only point of access to it is through illumination. The only panel painting to have survived was originally located in a choir chapel in Notre-Dame in Paris. It shows the large and wealthy Jouvenel des Ursins family, whose members, high-ranking officials at the French court, were closely involved in political events of the time. The work was originally intended as a diptych, with the figures pictured at prayer, looking towards some object of devotion that has since disappeared – in the same sort of composition as that used by Fouquet (see the diptych of Etienne Chevalier from Notre-Dame in Melun, the

87 Workshop of Peter Hemmel
of Andlau
Donor knight at prayer
Strasbourg, *c.* 1483
Stained glass

wings of which are now in Berlin and Antwerp). The size, the refined colours (gold, silver, red), and the relief brocades, combine to produce a luxurious celebration of this newly ennobled family. The spatial arrangement does not yet betray any Italian influence, and this probably indicates an outflow of artistic talent during the English occupation of Paris.

90 Italian techniques are also absent from the *Pietà* of Tarascon (so called because it is reputed to have come from the castle there). The dramatic scene of the dead Christ lying in his mother's arms – a scene typical of medieval spirituality – looks like a rather stiff rendering of the art of the great Flemish masters (Roger van der Weyden's *Deposition*, for example). The gold background, engraved with rinceaux, removes any suggestion of depth. But the monumentality of the composition, the use of the light

88 Battle scene. Page from the *Romuleon*, made by Benvenuto d'Imola for Charles of France
Eastern France, *c.* 1455–60
Illumination on parchment

89 Attributed to Jean Fouquet
Stained glass medallion with LG monogram
Paris (?), *c.* 1450–60

to model the forms, the restrained and refined handling, comparable to that of Enguerrand Quarton's masterpiece (in the Louvre), make this one of the finest examples of painting in Provence.

It is Jean Fouquet who must be credited with having synthesized the two aesthetic trends of Flemish realism and the Italian Renaissance. This occurred in mid-century, following Fouquet's stay in Italy. A circular painting *89* reminiscent of the small heraldic figures in the Book of Hours which Fouquet illustrated for Simon de Varie is notable for its great refinement. It bears the monogram LG of the patron who commissioned it, which may stand for Laurent Gyrard, secretary to Charles VII. Fouquet displayed his genius in portraiture, in landscape, and in history painting: his *Antiquités judaïques* were never equalled. The great account of Roman *88* history compiled by Benvenuto d'Imola, known as the *Romuleon*, inspired a whole series of illuminations. The Museum owns two leaves depicting an ancient town under siege. The design still owes something to the paradigms established at the beginning of the century by the Limburg brothers. The appearance of this type of illumination corresponded with a new taste amongst aristocratic bibliophiles of the fifteenth century, who, in a trend indicative of the times, were turning their attention to classical literature.

Engraving and printing played a major role in circulating the texts and *91* models used in all the visual arts. A *Carrying of the Cross*, the only fragment

90 'Tarascon Pietà' (detail)
Provence, before 1457
Panel painting

to have survived from the stained glass in the chapel of the Hôtel de Cluny – is based on a woodcut by Philippe Pigouchet, produced in Paris before 1500. Although the window is a product of the Normandy school, the fine interpretation and the quality of the workmanship none the less mark it out as the work of a virtuoso glass-painter.

In fact, the 1500s betray only very faint glimmers of the advances being made as part of the Italian Renaissance. This was the case, for example, at Abbeville, where every year – as in Amiens – the fraternity of Notre-Dame du Puy commissioned a painting. The *Virgin with the Wheat*, in *92*

which the Virgin is pictured between Louis XII and Pope Alexander VI and their retinues, is still very provincial and essentially Gothic in character, although it contains a number of realist details of Flemish inspiration and places the picture in an Italian-style architectural setting. The same is true of a leaf from a calendar, in which the balance between text and picture has been reversed in favour of the latter. It is also true of the great Castilian retable by the Master of Riofrio. Here, the depiction of *93* the death of Saint Martin is still static and archaic in style; but the introduction of Italian motifs and, more importantly, the quest for a new approach to space – albeit to accommodate figures that are still essentially Flemish in character – reveal the slow and steady penetration of Renaissance models.

S.L.

93 Master of Riofrio
Death of Saint Martin
Castile, *c.* 1500
Panel painting

92 *The Virgin with the Wheat* (detail)
Abbeville, early 16th century
Panel painting

91 *Carrying of the Cross*
Paris, chapel of the Hôtel de Cluny, *c.* 1500
Stained glass

Objets d'Art from the Thirteenth to the Beginning of the Sixteenth Century

Objets d'art were the domain *par excellence* in which medieval man gave expression to his religious faith. Indeed, most of the objects that have come down to us are religious works, in which extremely valuable materials – gold, silver, gems, ivory, enamels – are used to celebrate the wonders of God's creation.

Veneration of the saints and of their relics prompted many commissions. A shrine from the treasury of the cathedral in Moûtiers-en-Tarentaise *96* highlights the trading and artistic links that existed between the Eastern and Western worlds in the Middle Ages: it was created by an early thirteenth-century Western goldsmith using a casket in rock crystal made several centuries earlier in Egypt. Carving in rock crystal was a Fatimid speciality, and luxury items like jugs, cups, and caskets were made out of this precious material. Each of the four sides of the casket is engraved with an animal motif: the main facet shows two ibexes facing one another, with a floret in between; on the rear facet are two gazelles; and on the smaller facets a deer and a dog. The facets have all been quite skilfully recarved and then remounted in a framework of filigree, pearls, gems, and intaglios. An item of Islamic origin and secular purpose has thus been converted to religious use: the crystal plaques, despite their decoration, afforded a view of the relics preserved in the casket, now transformed into a shrine.

95 Reliquary from Our Lady's church, Dendermonde Flanders, *c.* 1220–30
Rock crystal, precious stones, silver gilt, niello

96 Shrine from the cathedral in Moûtiers-en-Tarentaise
Fatimid Egypt (?) and northern France, *c.* 1200
Rock crystal, silver gilt

The same concern to ensure visibility is evident in a six-lobed reliquary *95* from Flanders. The front side bears a fantastical openwork animal motif

94 *Virgin and Child*
Paris, *c.* 1250–60
Ivory

giving clear sight of the contents, and on the rear side is an enthroned figure of Christ flanked by two candlesticks. The filigree motif decorating the lobes is typical of the goldsmith's art in early thirteenth-century Flanders, displaying as it does Rhenish and Mosan influences.

Limoges

Goldsmith's work in the Rhenish and Mosan regions produced its finest creations in the twelfth century, and the Museum has only a few examples of later output. This is because Rhine and Meuse work was overtaken, in the thirteenth century, by *champlevé* enamel production from Limoges, also known as *œuvre de Limoges*. The Museum owns one of the

97 Three pyxes
Limoges, 13th century
Copper, *champlevé* enamel, gilding

98 Small reliquary of Saint Fausta
Limoges, mid-13th century
Copper, *champlevé* enamel, gilding

finest collections of this kind of enamelwork in the world, the core of which derives from the Du Sommerard collection, which has been steadily added to as the years passed. In addition to landmark items such as the figure of Christ from the former Spitzer collection, the Museum owns numerous works showing the diversity and range of Limoges production, from the most modest item upwards.

47

Champlevé enamel made its appearance in the south of Europe in the second half of the twelfth century and developed extremely rapidly during the thirteenth. At the Lateran Council of 1215, Innocent III approved its use in sacred vessels. Limoges enamel then entered a period of what was virtually mass production, supplying liturgical objects to the whole of the Western world, including Italy and Sweden. One of the chief reasons for its popularity was that it provided colour and opulence at relatively modest cost, since the basic material used was gilded copper. Limoges goldsmiths became major suppliers of shrines. These all take the same form – a house with a saddleback roof – but their size varies, as does their decoration, part of which is usually devoted to the life of the saint concerned. The Museum owns two shrines of Saint Fausta, a fourth-century martyr much venerated in Aquitaine. On the larger shrine, one facet depicts scenes from the life of the saint, with figures in reserves against a background of stylized flowerets; the other facet is decorated with figures in relief. (To speed up and simplify production, sets of figurines in *mezzo relievo* were prepared in advance, ready to be applied to a particular object.) On the smaller shrine dedicated to Saint Fausta, the arrangement *98* is reversed: the scenes from the saint's life are made up of *appliqué* figures, and the angels on the back are depicted in reserves on an enamelled background.

The Museum's very rich collections illustrate the full range of liturgical implements as produced in the workshops of Limoges: precious bindings for Gospel books (for example, two boards which, very unusually, still *99* have their original wooden supports), crosses, candlesticks, censers, and pyxes. These latter were designed to hold consecrated Eucharistic hosts *97* and were usually made in the shape of a small round box topped with a conical lid and cross. Sometimes they took the more elaborate form of a Eucharistic dove, the body of which served as a container for hosts. The *100* dove was hung above the altar, thus indicating symbolically that the Holy Spirit was present in the church.

As well as engaging in this more routine production, the workshops of Limoges produced a number of higher-quality items. One such is a reli- *101* quary cross decorated with gems and a delicate network of filigree. The two transverse sections are typical of the reliquaries of the True Cross that began to appear in great numbers after the capture of Constantinople by the Crusaders in 1204. The relics were housed in small lozenge-shaped compartments set in the stem and the arms of the reliquary.

99 Book boards depicting the Salvator Mundi and the Crucifixion
Limoges, 1st quarter 13th century
Copper, *champlevé* enamel, gilding

Precious Works of Art during the Reign of Louis IX

During Saint Louis's reign, Paris was one of the great artistic centres of the Western world. In the courtly circle that formed around the king, the nobility mingled with the wealthy bourgeoisie, and this brought a growth in the clientele for works of art. The goldsmith's craft became better organized and began to flourish. First amongst the patrons, however, was Louis IX himself, and the expansion in courtly art centred mainly round royal commissions.

Sumptuous reliquaries were created to contain the relics of the Passion which Saint Louis had bought from the emperor of Constantinople Baudouin of Flanders and which were kept in the Sainte-Chapelle. They were incorporated into one huge reliquary, the *Grande Châsse* (Great Shrine), and exposed in a special gallery. The whole sacred display was destroyed during the Revolution, but for some reason that is not clear, one reliquary miraculously survived the depredations, and it entered the Museum's collections in 1881. The relics it contains are not of the Passion but of Saints Lucian, Julian, and Maxian, who brought the Gospel to the Beauvais area. Saint Louis is known to have attended the translation of the relics in Beauvais in 1261, and it was probably on this occasion that these particular fragments were removed and given to the king. The reliquary created to house them is a good illustration of the kind of art fostered in Paris under Saint Louis's patronage: three blind arcades rhythmically span each side of the tiny building; their shape and that of

102

100 Eucharistic dove
Limoges, 1st third of 13th century
Copper, *champlevé* enamel, gilding

101 Reliquary cross of the True Cross
Limousin region, 2nd half 13th century
Gilded copper

the crocket capitals echo those of the Sainte-Chapelle and, more particularly, the design of the baldachin over the gallery containing the relics. One side has three glazed openings in it, through which the relics can be seen; on the other side are the figures of the three saints as *cephalophores*. These chased silver figures are reminiscent of Parisian sculptures of the 1260s, such as those in the southern arm of the transept in Notre-Dame. Each of the faces bears a different expression, ranging from the asceticism of Bishop Lucian to the handsome serenity and youthfulness of Saint Julian. The formal rigour and delicate execution endow the figures with extraordinary physical presence, and provide a rare testimony to the skill of the Parisian goldsmiths in the 1260s. The reliquary of Saint Lucian provides a very typical example of the way in which architecture

102 Reliquary of Saints Lucian, Julian, and Maxian, from the Sainte-Chapelle, Paris, 1261–2
Repoussé silver, chased and gilded

influenced precious objects in the second half of the thirteenth century, resulting in the production of what are virtually miniature buildings in gold and silver.

The art of the ivory carver developed alongside that of the goldsmith at the French royal court. Having become very difficult to obtain during the Romanesque period, elephant ivory began to reappear on the European trading circuit in the thirteenth century and was much sought after as material for making precious objects. Parisian ivory-carvers produced all sorts of items intended for devotional use, notably statuettes, either singly or in groups, and particularly statuettes of the Virgin and Child. The Virgin is most often depicted seated, with the Child on her knee. Sometimes she is standing, as is the case in a very large figure of the Virgin in which the pose and strong slant of the hips follows the line of the tusk. Despite their size, these small statues conform in all respects to sculptural criteria: with their slanting hips and voluminous drapery with wide intersecting folds, they are closely akin to the monumental sculptures which adorned the cathedrals at that time. The interchange between the monumental and the decorative arts during this period was continual and particularly fruitful.

104 These links are discernible in a triptych from Saint-Sulpice du Tarn, dating from the period spanning the end of the thirteenth and beginning of the fourteenth century. In the central panel, the figures in high relief – particularly those of the Virgin and the two angels – resemble portal sculptures. On the wings the figures are flatter, heralding the trend of fourteenth-century ivory-carving towards low-relief work on diptychs, triptychs, and mirror-leaves rather than work 'in the round'.

103 Seal-ring belonging to Guillaume de Flouri
Italy (?), late 13th century
Gold, amethyst

104 Triptych from Saint-Sulpice du Tarn
Parisian workshop, late 13th century
Polychrome painting on ivory

Jewellery and Ornaments

Besides the very rich collections of religious goldsmith's work, the Museum boasts a rare set of secular items of this kind, including various pieces of jewellery ranging from the modest to the sumptuous. A recent *103* acquisition – a seal-ring belonging to Guillaume de Flouri (his name is carved around the bezel) – plunges us into the world of the Crusades. Guillaume belonged to a family that had settled in the Holy Land in the twelfth century, and he was viscount of Acre (Akko) from 1274 to 1277. At that time, Acre was one of the last outposts of the Crusaders; it fell to the Muslims some twenty years later. Guillaume was an important figure in the retinue of Hugues de Lusignan, King of Cyprus and Jerusalem. The three-faceted ring bears a 'magic' inscription: 'Guggug Balte Bani Ezera Ezera Ezerave Lagain AO'. Such inscriptions are common on the jewellery of the fourteenth and fifteenth centuries and had a prophylactic function: they were believed to protect the wearer from toothache and attacks of epilepsy or gout.

105 A very rare set of filigree enamels – *émaux de plique* – provides a dazzling example of the skill of the Parisian goldsmith. These small-scale ornaments were made by soldering delicate gold wires onto a sheet of gold and filling the resulting spaces with enamel. Translucent green was used for the background; opaque blue, red, and white for the design. It is from this complicated – *plicatus* – pattern that the term *plique* is supposed to derive. These decorative items may have been used on ceremonial clothing (those in the Museum have small hooks on the side, making it possible to sew them onto material) or on religious objects: we know that the reliquary bust of Saint Louis commissioned by Philippe le Bel was

105 Guillaume Julien (?)
Six gems in setting
Paris, *c.* 1300
Translucent and opaque
cloisonné enamel

adorned with a row of filigree enamels of this kind. The goldsmith from whom the king commissioned the bust, Guillaume Julien, specialized in this type of work, and it became extremely popular in the period at the end of the thirteenth and beginning of the fourteenth century. Other Parisian goldsmiths imitated him, and filigree enamels were sold far beyond the confines of Paris, and indeed of France.

A collection of items found in 1863 gives us an impression of goldsmith's work in the mid-fourteenth century. The treasure was discovered in the wall of a house in the former Jewish quarter of Colmar. The coins which it contains indicate its age and provenance: they come from Basle and date from the 1330s. The presence of a Jewish wedding-ring, recognizable by its shape and by the good-luck inscription set into the enamel in Hebrew characters, would seem to indicate that the treasure was hidden by a Jewish person fleeing the pogroms that erupted in the Rhine region during the Black Death of 1348–9. Was he himself a goldsmith, or was he simply a pawnbroker? The items which he hid show the range of wares on offer to a client seeking to embellish his own or his wife's appearance: belts decorated with little ornaments in silver; applied ornaments for sewing onto clothes; a clasp decorated with precious stones; and, of course, rings, either in silver or, more often, gold, adorned with precious or semi-precious stones and in many cases very finely worked – like the one with an onyx set between two clasped hands, or the one with a sapphire framed with small stylized dragons' heads.

The Cult of Relics

During the fourteenth century, artistic centres began to proliferate around the princely courts. Having become the papal residence in 1309, Avignon assumed a major artistic role. The pope, the cardinals, and their court were all potential patrons of the arts. They attracted artists to the city, and Avignon became an artistic crossroads, acting as a staging-post in particular for new Italian ideas. One of the Museum's masterpieces – the *Golden Rose* – was commissioned by Pope John XXII from a Sienese artist resident in Avignon, Minucchio da Siena. Every year on the fourth Sunday in Lent, the pope gave a golden rose to a person he wished to honour. The papal accounts and the coat of arms on the mounting indicate that this particular rose was given in 1330 to the count of Neufchâtel, Rudolf III, an ally of the pope's in his dispute with Ludwig of Bavaria.

Sienese goldsmith's work was also notable in the fourteenth century for its revival of enamelling techniques. After the success of Limoges *champlevé*, tastes shifted towards a technique known as *basse-taille*, in which translucent enamels were applied to engraved metal – usually silver. Using a range of delicate colours – greens, oranges, greys, purples, bronzes – the Sienese goldsmiths harnessed the effects of light in these small engraved plaques, which were used to decorate chalices, crosses, and reliquaries of various shapes. The Museum owns several works of this kind: a reliquary monstrance, a chalice, a reliquary of Saint Galganus, and a number of plaques detached from their original supports. The Sienese technique became very popular and inspired many other Italian goldsmiths, and did so right up to the fifteenth century, as is indicated by a large processional cross from central Italy. The extremities are decorated with squat figures in *ronde-bosse*, contrasting with the brightly coloured little enamel plaques set like veritable stained-glass windows in the arms.

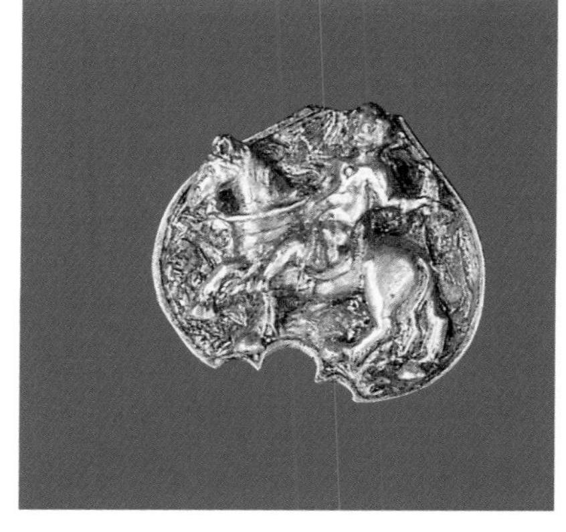

106 Brooch
France or Rhineland,
1st third of 14th century
Silver, partly gilded

107 Jewish wedding-ring
Early 14th century
Gold, enamel, filigree

Rings from the Colmar treasury. Lower Rhineland, mid-14th century
Gold

Basse-taille enamelling also became popular in Spain, at the courts of Catalonia and Aragon. A fine processional cross in silver has ends *112* shaped like fleur-de-lis bearing enamelled quatre-foils decorated with figures of angels. Their green, yellow, and purple colouring against a background of bright blue produces an acid palette reminiscent of Sienese enamels. The cross bears a Barcelona hallmark at various points, reflecting the custom that grew up during the fourteenth century of having the stamp of the originating city applied to gold and silver items. In France, Jean le Bon decreed in 1355 that such pieces must bear a master goldsmith's mark.

Parisian artists had also adopted the *basse-taille* technique for both religious and secular items. Their creations sometimes resembled miniature

109 Pietro Vannini (?)
Cross
Central Italy, 2nd half 15th century
Silver gilt, translucent enamel

paintings – as is the case with a reliquary pendant of Saint Genevieve. *110* On the front, set in a framework of foliage, is a scene depicting an event during the siege of Paris by Attila: as Saint Genevieve made her way, candle in hand, to take provisions to the besieged inhabitants, a wicked little devil would blow out the candle, and an angel would repeatedly come and light it again. The decoration of punched foliage forms a delicate background to this lively little cameo. On the reverse side, a sliding panel engraved with a peacock protects the relics of the patron saint of Paris.

108 Minucchio da Siena
Golden rose given by Pope John XXII to Rudolf of Nidau
Avignon, 1330
Gold

110 Reliquary of Saint Genevieve
Paris, *c.* 1380
Silver gilt, translucent enamel

111 Reliquary clasp with eagle motif
Bohemia (?), mid-14th century
Silver gilt

In many objects of this period, the dividing-line between the sacred and the secular becomes increasingly difficult to determine. A great reliquary clasp from Bohemia, like the reliquary picture of Saint Genevieve, is an accessory for clothing: it has a ceremonial, and therefore social, function, but it also has a religious one, given the relics it houses. At the centre of a four-lobed container holding the relics is set a gilded and engraved silver lozenge figuring a magnificent eagle with gem-studded wings. This may be the symbol of the Holy Roman Empire, and the clasp may have belonged to the Emperor Charles IV, an enthusiastic collector of relics. It could, however, equally well have been used to fix the vestments of some high-ranking clergyman. *111*

The period of International Gothic, between the end of the fourteenth and beginning of the fifteenth century, saw the appearance of a new trend, that of opaque enamel painted onto gold. This was the age of lavish courts, of princely contacts and gift-giving that cemented dynastic and family ties and led to the establishment of the same highly refined life-style across the whole of Europe. A Virgin and Child reliquary intended to house a fragment of the umbilical cord of Christ illustrates the typical features of this delicate style. The flesh-tones were originally picked out in colour, of which only a few traces survive. The figure came from the treasury of Notre-Dame-en-Vaux (Marne) and was commissioned, probably from a Parisian goldsmith, by the executors of the will of a wealthy member of the bourgeoisie in Châlons-sur-Marne. *113*

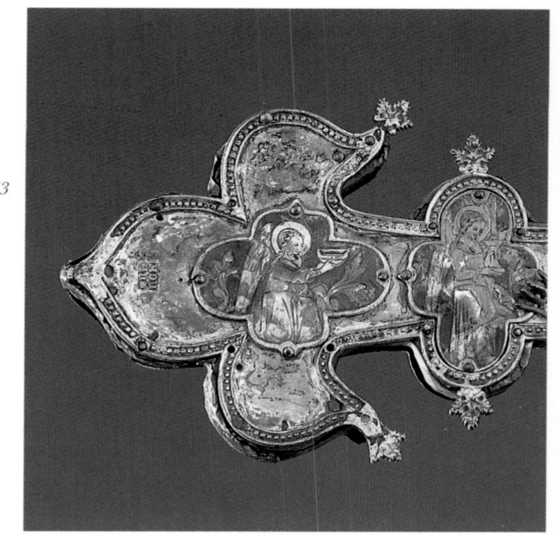

112 Cross (detail)
Barcelona, 3rd quarter 14th century
Silver gilt, translucent enamel

The cult of the saints, and particularly of their relics, reached its high point at the end of the Middle Ages, and the Museum's collections provide a full account of this period. Reliquaries proliferated and began to appear in a variety of shapes. Traditional examples, in which the reliquary was given the shape of the part of the body from which the relic derived – arm, foot, etc. – continued to be made; but the tendency now was to try to display the relic itself, through the use of cylindrical containers or glass sections. The reliquary was thus transformed into a monstrance, often in the shape of a fantastical Flamboyant-style structure with miniature pinnacles, bell-towers, and statues. *114*

These lavishly decorated monstrances were made in particularly large numbers in Germanic areas, where the goldsmith's art underwent a period of extraordinary development at the end of the Middle Ages. In commercial centres where wealthy merchants provided a reliable clientele, the number of goldsmiths greatly increased: there were 122 of them in Cologne in 1395. Names in this period begin to be better known, because the craftsmen sign their work more often than previously. A figure of Saint Anne in gilded and painted silver, for example, bears, on the back of the throne, the name of the person who commissioned it, the date of the work, the name of the artist, and the sum paid for it! The theme of the three generations, in which Saint Anne is pictured with both the Virgin Mary (depicted as a child) and the Infant Jesus on her lap, was a favourite one amongst German artists of the late Middle Ages, and there are numerous carved, painted, and engraved versions of it. The development of engraving – first on wood and later on copper – and also, ultimately, of printing, was due in part to the industry and enthusiasm of the silversmiths and goldsmiths. *115*

E.A.

DE UMBILICO DOMINI JESU CHRISTI

115 Hanns Greiff
Reliquary statue of the Virgin
and Child with Saint Anne
Ingolstadt, 1472
Painted and gilded silver

114 Reliquary monstrance (detail)
Germany, early 16th century
Silver gilt

113 Reliquary statue
of the umbilical cord of Christ
from the collegiate church
of Notre-Dame-en-Vaux,
Châlons-sur-Marne
Paris (?), 1407
Silver gilt

MON SEVL DESIR

Textile Art from the Thirteenth to the Beginning of the Sixteenth Century

Oriental and Western Textiles

The Museum's remarkable collection of ancient textiles reflects the various modes of manufacture and decoration that prevailed at various times from Antiquity to the end of the Middle Ages, and highlights the great centres of production. Oriental fabrics from Iran, Egypt, and the Byzantine empire rub shoulders with products from the Western world. There is such a wealth of holdings that only a small proportion can be displayed, for reasons both of space and of conservation. This stock of treasures derives from a number of major collectors – Stanislas Baron, Adolphe de Rothschild, Marcel Guérin, Claudius Côte. There are also some items from prestigious historical sources, such as the Sainte-Chapelle treasury, the excavations in Saint-Germain-des-Prés, the treasuries of Saint-Sernin in Toulouse and Saint-Mexme in Chinon.
Trade in textiles, like that in goldsmith's work, was one of the liveliest branches of commerce in the Middle Ages. We know how much Byzantine silks were sought after in the Carolingian age and in fifteenth-century Italy; we know how important the great Champagne fairs were for the cloth-merchants, and what wealth the wool-traders brought to Flanders. Until the end of the Romanesque period, only fabrics of a functional nature were produced in the West, and high-quality textiles from the Orient were therefore in great demand, not only for use in the manufacture of clothing for the upper classes, but also as a means of expressing religious devotion. In the Church, precious fabrics were used for a great variety of purposes. Evidence of their use in decoration and furnishing has come down to us largely through pictorial and other representations, whereas, in the case of liturgical vestments, a number of actual examples have survived. None the less, it is still difficult to determine the exact origin and place of manufacture of many of the textiles that have been preserved.
The Byzantine court, the gateway to the Orient, was a nerve-centre of the silk-trade. The most lavish fabrics were those produced by the imperial workshops. These were discovered enfolding relics in tombs or holy treasure-houses, and they served as models and references throughout the Middle Ages.
Byzantine influence also percolated to Italy, either directly or through the medium of Hispano-Moorish textiles. Great Italian cities such as Siena, Lucca, and Florence, became very active centres of silk production from as early as the thirteenth century. Motifs of monsters, birds, front-to-front lions, and rings were used more or less freely and imaginatively. A pontifical stocking would seem to have been made in Lucca. *117*
The material, green silk brocade, dates from the thirteenth century and bears a decoration of front-to-front eagles and antelopes, some of the details of which are picked out in gold thread. The stocking was found in

117 Pontifical stocking belonging to Cardinal Arnaud de Via
Lucca, Italy, 13th century
Silk brocade with gold thread

116 *The Lady and the Unicorn: A mon seul désir* (detail)
Southern Netherlands, after Parisian cartoon, between 1484 and 1500
Tapestry in wool and silk

the nineteenth century in the binding of a cartulary in the abbey of Villeneuve-les-Avignon. Its owner may have been Arnaud de Via, a nephew of Pope John XXII, who resided at the papal court in Avignon, was appointed cardinal in 1317, and died in 1335. From as early as the end of the fourteenth century, sumptuous velvets rivalling those of the Orient were being woven in Italy: Florence, Genoa, and Venice were producing some magnificent fabric, and the Museum has a number of fine examples, most of them from liturgical vestments such as copes and chasubles. A warm red velvet forms the background to the stunning *Broderie aux Léopards* (Leopard Embroidery). Sewn into a chasuble during the seventeenth century, the fabric is decorated with embroidered leopards shimmering with silver thread, cabochons, and pearls. The elegant monsters, with coats of spiralled gold thread, tongues hanging out, and brows in high relief, encircling eyes picked out with glass cabochons, cannot fail to fascinate. Amongst luxuriant foliage embroidered with silver thread, a host of figures, old and young, are depicted at play, recreating a refined and courtly world. The large fragments are believed to come from a ceremonial horse-cloth used at the court of Edward III of

118

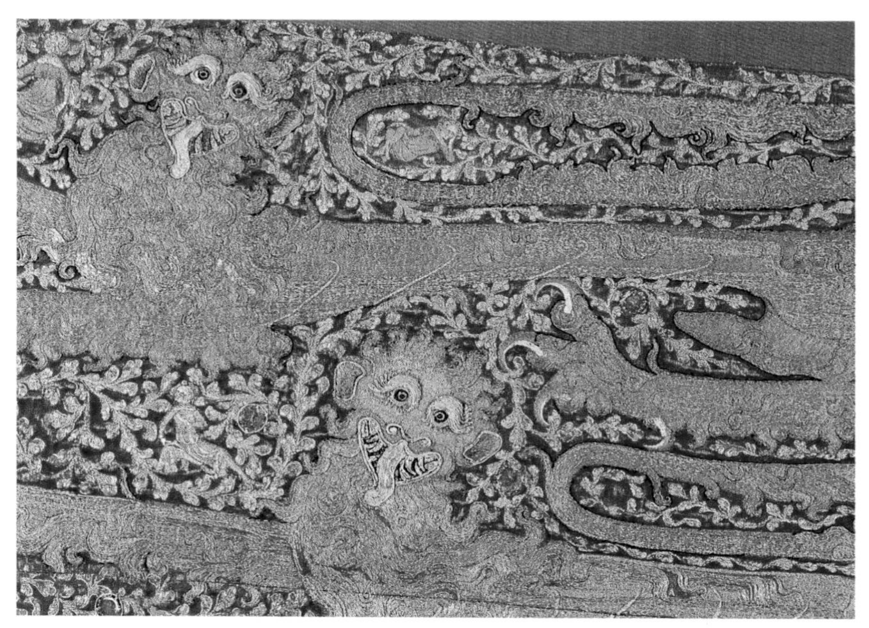

118 'Leopard Embroidery'
England, 1st third 14th century
Embroidery in silk, silver thread, cabochons, and pearls on velvet

England (1327–77). The style and technique indicate English workmanship. English production was so prolific and its success so remarkable, that the term *opus anglicanum* rapidly gained currency, even though the exact technique which it implies cannot be defined precisely.

Other items of embroidery illustrate particular regional trends. In addition to England, the Rhine valley, particularly the region around Cologne, was notable for its high-quality products. An embroidered fragment depicting Saint John the Evangelist under a series of arches was originally part of an altar-frontal, now divided up, from the monastery of Huysburg, near Halberstadt, in Lower Saxony. It is embroidered in silk thread on linen, and would appear, from the architectural decor and style of the figures, to have been produced in the monastery workshop during the 1150s. The same ornamental architectural features are present on an altar-frontal depicting scenes from the lives of Saints Mark, John, and Martin. It is a sumptuous piece of embroidery betraying both Rhenish and, more particularly, Mosan influences. Its provenance – the civil hospital in Mechelen – is confirmed by

49

119 Purse belonging to the 'Countess of Bar'
France, 14th century
Embroidery on silk with metal thread and silk

120 Orphrey of Manassès and Ermengarde
France, late 13th century
Embroidery on linen with metal thread and silk

an early source, and its iconography is extremely original. The style of the figures and of the architecture reflects artistic trends at the start of the fourteenth century.

Orphreys were long embroidered bands applied to liturgical vestments such as chasubles and copes. They depicted scenes from the Bible or the lives of the saints. One example, a delicately embroidered item in gold *120* thread dating from the thirteenth century and beautifully preserved, comes from the abbey of Vergy in Burgundy. It depicts the ninth-century founders of the abbey, Count Manassès and his consort, Ermengarde, dedicating their church to the Virgin. The embroidery, in the form of a large rectangle, was sewn into a chasuble which, according to the archives, was made by the monk Pierre, who is believed to be pic-

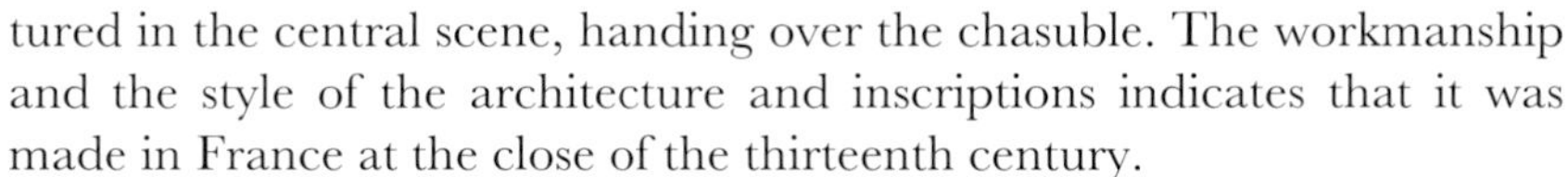

tured in the central scene, handing over the chasuble. The workmanship and the style of the architecture and inscriptions indicates that it was made in France at the close of the thirteenth century.

Medieval sources indicate that there were centres of textile production all over Europe: London, Antwerp, Venice, Paris. The demand for wall-hangings and frontals, and for liturgical and ceremonial vestments, resulted in a prolific output. *Aumonières* or purses were a popular female accessory, and their embroidered decoration is often of high quality. Amongst the many purses on display at the Museum, the one from the abbey of Saint-Mihiel in Lorraine is original in having a secular design *119* of jesters and grotesques. Made of green silk highlighted with metal thread, it is the product of a Parisian workshop and is believed to have belonged to a countess of Bar. Two fourteenth-century mitres, rare from the point of view both of the material of which they are made (silk) and of their origins (the Sainte-Chapelle treasury), provide sumptuous examples of French workmanship. The first of these, painted in black on white *121* silk, emulates painting, whilst the second, with its embroidered padding, seed-pearls, glass beads, and filigree enamel, now lost, attempts to rival the goldsmith's art. The latter mitre, in silk damask, bears a very elabo- *123* rate architectural and floral design in gold thread which the ancient inventories termed *en tabernacle*. Its shape and the decorative and architectural features indicate it was made in Paris at the end of the fourteenth century. The painted mitre, for use at times of mourning or in Lent,

121 Embroidered mitre from the treasury of the Sainte-Chapelle Paris (?), 14th century Embroidery on silk with metal thread and pearls

depicts the Entombment of Christ and the Resurrection in Indian ink on white silk, in a Rayonnant-style architectural setting. The lappets are also painted: one figures the Holy Virgin, the other the treasurer-dean of the Sainte-Chapelle, separated by elaborate architectural canopies.

The stylistic affinities between the decoration of the mitre and the output of Parisian painters in the middle of the fourteenth century are very clear. It is an extremely rare piece and reminds one of the great silk wall-hanging in *grisaille*, known as the *Parement de Narbonne*, commissioned by King Charles v and his consort, Jeanne, and now housed in the Musée du Louvre.

Reminiscent of embroidered work both in its lavishness and in its pictorial style inspired by Flemish models, the *Resurrection Tapestry*, worked entirely in silk and metal thread, is a masterpiece of Arras craftsmanship. *122*

It may have been commissioned by the wealthy archbishop of Zaragoza, who died in 1454. Another fragment of this altar-frontal, illustrating the Deposition, is housed in the Victoria and Albert Museum in London.

A small panel illustrating the healing of the blind woman at the tomb of Saint Martin indicates the close links between painting and the decorative arts. This work of refined draughtsmanship and subtle harmonies of colour is the work of Pierre du Billant, a master-embroiderer of German origin, working from a drawing by Barthélemy d'Eyck, painter and valet to René d'Anjou. The panel was originally part of a *chapelle* (set of liturgical vestments) honouring Saint Martin of Tours and donated by King René during the 1440s. *124*

The other medallions and panels are scattered amongst various American and French museums. René was renowned as a patron of the arts and as an artist, and both Barthélemy d'Eyck and Pierre du Billant were attached to his court. Their frequent appearance in the royal accounts indicate the degree of artistic interchange that took place between different princely centres.

123 Painted mitre from the treasury of Sainte-Chapelle, Paris, *c.* 1350–70
Indian ink on silk

122 Altar-hanging depicting the Resurrection
Arras, *c.* 1420
Tapestry in silk and metal thread

Medieval Tapestry

From the time of its creation in 1843, the Museum owned a number of items of tapestry, including the very fine *Deliverance of Saint Peter*. The Museum quickly consolidated its reputation by acquiring other exceptional pieces such as the *David and Bathsheba* wall-hanging, purchased in 1847 and now in the Musée National de la Renaissance at Ecouen. It was between 1880 and 1882 that Edmond Du Sommerard made his two finest acquisitions in this area: the *Life of Saint Stephen* and the *Lady and the Unicorn* tapestries. The degree of interest in this branch of art was also reflected in the publication, in both France and Germany, of major studies on medieval tapestry. In recent years, the Museum has made a number of further acquisitions, such as that of the tapestry of *Lérian and Lauréolle*, and it has also published several works on tapestry, thus confirming the curators' continuing interest in this prestigious section of the Museum's collection.

Technique and Production Centres

Tapestry is a re-creation, in wool, silk, and sometimes gold and silver, of a full-size model – the cartoon. It was closely linked to the art of its time, particularly miniature and panel painting, and as a mural decoration, it provided warmth and cheered the eye. It was woven by hand on a loom. Painters as such do not seem to have been called on very frequently to produce the designs, and only a few documents record the names of the artists who did make the cartoons that were then handed to the weavers. The more general opinion is that the workshops owned stocks of sketches taken from engravings or other tapestries, and that these were then adapted by specially trained craftsmen from the same workshop.

17 *18* *21* The oldest pieces of tapestry at Cluny date from the Coptic age and were made by Christian craftsmen in Egypt between the fourth and eleventh centuries. They were preserved in tombs. Of very high quality, they originally adorned the front of clothing, in which tapestry and fabric were woven in a single piece. Their most delightful feature is their stylized look, resulting from the combination of pure colour, subtle technique, and great freedom of expression.

Medieval tapestries, meanwhile, given the surfaces they were intended to cover and the resources they required, had different objectives. Closely bound up with princely patronage, they were, like the goldsmith's art, also, and above all, a means of asserting status, wealth, and power. In the fourteenth century, the workshops of Paris – those we know of – were very active. Between 1377 and 1380, Nicolas Bataille, a Parisian merchant, managed to supply all six tapestries of the famous series of the *Apocalypse* for the Duc d'Anjou (which can be seen in the château at Angers), a variety of historiated hangings for Charles VI, his wife, Isabel of Bavaria, and his brother, Louis d'Orléans, and – in 1395 alone – five wall-hangings for the duke of Burgundy.

124 *The Miracle of Saint Martin*
Southern Netherlands, after a cartoon by Barthélemy d'Eyck, *c.* 1440
Orphrey embroidered with gold thread and silk

125 In the Alemannic and Germanic areas, tapestry developed as a form of decoration for furnishings. An example of its use as a cushion for a bed or sofa is provided by a small tapestry in wool and linen depicting two loving couples against a background of stylized foliage and flowers. Brightly coloured tapestries of this kind date from the end of the fifteenth century and were based on woodcuts circulating in the Rhine area at that time. In the provinces of Flanders and Artois, which had a tradition of textile manufacture, weaving workshops began to shift over to the production of luxury items. These woven walls, designed as huge, movable decorations, served as symbols of princely status or as lavish gifts. During the fifteenth century, Tournai was a major production centre, from which important merchants and workshop owners such as Arnold Poissonier supplied tapestries to the dukes of Burgundy. By about 1500, Brussels had become the main textile centre in the Netherlands, selling its products to all the courts and aristocratic houses of Europe. The markedly decorative role of some of these pieces is illustrated by a tapestry depicting *Seigneurial Life*. Bought by Edmond Du Sommerard in 1852 from a noble family in Rouen, it comprises six sections illustrating the life of a lord and his lady in about 1500. It is woven in wool and exemplifies the *mille-fleurs* ('thousand-flowers') style. The dark blue background is strewn with clumps of small flowers and trees. Amidst this luxuriant vegetation are a number of richly adorned figures essentially unconnected with one another. They are not looking at one another, and their feet do not seem to be touching the ground. The rather uninspiring impression evoked by these tapestries is explained by the weavers' habit of reusing cartoons, either altering or reversing them. A case in point is that of the lady-in-waiting, depicted first in the *Bath* tapestry and again, with a few modifications to clothing and hairstyle, in the hanging called *Strolling*. One of the commonest sources of inspiration for cartoon designers was engraving. The figure of the halberdier in the *Departure for the* 126 *Hunt*, for example, is taken from a Dürer engraving entitled *The Six Warriors*; and the same engraving served as inspiration both for the *Miracle of Saint Julian* in the Louvre and for a tapestry now in the Art Institute in Chicago. A similar diversity of inspiration is visible from the point of view of style. In the *Bath*, a naked young woman is submerged in a bathtub whose acanthus and lion's-head decoration is reminiscent of Renais-

125 *Loving Couples*
Upper Rhineland,
3rd quarter 15th century
Tapestry in wool and linen

sance art, whereas the hairstyles and the clothing, with its angular drapery, are typical of the Southern Netherlands at the end of the fifteenth century. The style of presentation chosen by the Museum is in perfect keeping with the tapestry, re-creating as it does a 'tapestry chamber' of 144 the kind evoked in the inventories of castles and mansion-houses.

The well-to-do clientele which bought these items was also fond of 'genre scenes', depicting shepherds, woodcutters, and grape-pickers. In the tapestry of the *Grape Harvest*, for example, the workers pursue their 127, 158 traditional occupations under the watchful eye of a seigneurial couple. The realistic details – tools, clothing, poses – are an invaluable source of historical information.

Tapestries depicting religious themes were as highly valued as those with secular subjects and might well be found in private houses. Stories from the Old and New Testament also provided the subject matter for huge woven epics of a kind in which the cities of Flanders and the Southern Netherlands – Arras, Lille, Brussels, Tournai – specialized. The parable of the Prodigal Son provided the subject matter for an elaborate tapestry 128 of which only the fragment in the Museum survives. The 'thousand flowers' scattered across the lower part complement an undulating landscape dotted with castles, palaces, and genre scenes. A tapestry illustrating *Arithmetic* is the only one to have survived from a set depicting the liberal 129 arts. A young woman is doing her accounts seated at a 'linenfold' table; the young men surrounding her, in a rather disorderly fashion, are wearing billowing clothes with wide collars and rather contrived folds. One of the figures appears in both parts, once in reverse. Other tapestries in the Musée des Arts Décoratifs in Paris and in the Museums of Boston and Göteborg have similar figures in them, adapted from a single set of cartoons. Like the *Prodigal Son*, these two pieces were made in the workshops of Tournai and evoke the same artistic milieu of the early sixteenth century. One of the Museum's recent acquisitions consists of three pieces

127 *The Grape Harvest* (detail)
Southern Netherlands,
early 16th century
Tapestry in wool and silk

126 *Seigneurial Life: The Departure for the Hunt*
Southern Netherlands, *c.* 1520
Tapestry in wool and silk

from an unusual series. The *Story of Lérian and Lauréolle* is based on a late *130* fifteenth-century Spanish novel and points to a source of inspiration dear to the hearts of cartoon designers and weavers, namely great historical novels, which were much in vogue with their wealthy, educated clientele. The composition, the style of the figures, the clothing all have their origins in Flemish painting of the first quarter of the sixteenth century.

Choir Hangings

Large-scale narrative religious tapestries were generally hung over choir stalls. As well as excluding draughts, they enlivened and fuelled the prayers of the monks or canons. Most of a tapestry relating the *Story of Saint* *131*

Peter, donated by Guillaume de Hellande, bishop of Beauvais, to his church in 1461, remains in the cathedral treasury. The fragment owned by the Museum is identified by the coats of arms of the cathedral chapter and of the bishop, and by the latter's motto: 'Peace'. The style of the work, with its easy draughtsmanship and tranquil poses, is reminiscent of the work of Jacques Daret, a pupil of Robert Campin, who was active in Tournai. The other choir tapestry on display at the Museum is exceptional from the point of view both of its state of preservation and of the historical interest attaching to it. Forty-five metres in length, it depicts the *Life of Saint Stephen* *132, 133* in a comic-strip-like series of twelve sections woven in wool and silk. The iconography is drawn mainly from the Golden Legend, a 'life of the saints' compiled by Jacobus de Voragine, bishop of Genoa, in the thirteenth century. As well as relating the saint's life, the tapestry devotes space to the miracles that happened after his death, and to the peregrinations undergone by his relics on their way to Rome. It was commissioned at some time in the 1500s by Jean Baillet, bishop of Auxerre, for his cathedral, and it is of great interest for its iconography, the quality of its figures, and its historical content. Scenes set in landscapes alternate with scenes set indoors, and the whole narrative has a realistic air. Each section carries an explanatory text set in cartouches. The composition, the poses, and some details of clothing are reminiscent of Brussels style. Hung in the chapel and its adjoining rooms at the Museum, above choir stalls from a church in Beauvais, the tapestry occupies a prime position.

130 *Lérian and Lauréolle* (detail)
Southern Netherlands,
early 16th century
Tapestry in wool and silk

129 *Arithmetic* (detail)
Tournai, *c.* 1500
Tapestry in wool and silk

128 *The Departure of the Prodigal Son* (detail)
Tournai, *c.* 1520
Tapestry in wool and silk

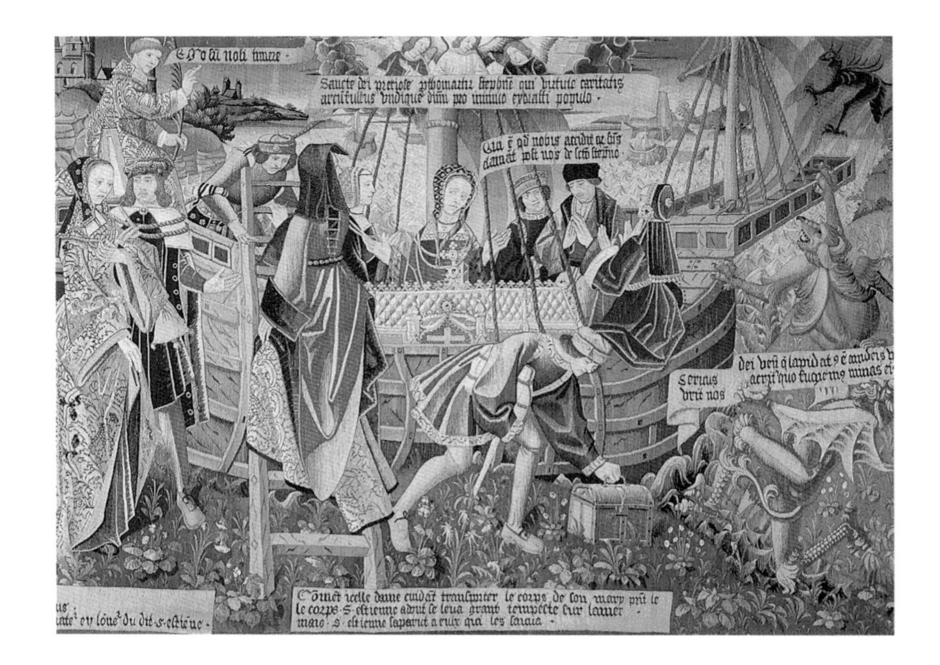

131 *The Deliverance of Saint Peter* (detail)
Tapestry from Beauvais cathedral
Tournai, 1460
Tapestry in wool and silk

132 *The Life of Saint Stephen* (detail)
Tapestry from Auxerre cathedral
Brussels, *c.* 1500
Tapestry in wool and silk

133 *The Life of Saint Stephen* (detail)

134 *The Lady and the Unicorn: Taste* (detail)
Southern Netherlands, after Parisian cartoon, between 1484 and 1500
Tapestry in wool and silk

135 *The Lady and the Unicorn: Hearing* (detail)

Pages 108–109:

136 *The Lady and the Unicorn: A mon seul désir* (detail)

137 *The Lady and the Unicorn: Taste* (detail)

138 *The Lady and the Unicorn: A mon seul désir* (detail)

The Lady and the Unicorn

The series of the *Lady and the Unicorn* is deservedly famous. Its mysterious discovery in the château at Boussac (Creuse) by the novelist George Sand in 1844 has lent it an air of legend, and it continues to dazzle visitors with its charm and poetry. However, its existence had already been noted in 1841 by Prosper Mérimée, then Inspecteur des Monuments Historiques, who expressed concern about its conservation. Edmond du Sommerard finally managed to acquire it for the Museum in 1882, and it is one of its most precious exhibits. Recent research has clarified the circumstances in which the set was commissioned, but the archives give no indication of the name of the cartoon designer or the place of manufacture. The person who commissioned the work is identified by his coat of arms: gules a bend azure charged with three crescents argent. This was evidently repeated on each section using two heraldic animals – the lion and the unicorn.

A mythological animal with the body of a goat, the head of a horse, and a single horn in the shape of a narwhal's tusk, the unicorn, which was reputed to be extremely strong and fast, could only be captured by a young woman. It was frequently represented in medieval iconography where it occurs in both religious and secular contexts (Christ/lover). For Jean Le Viste, a wealthy lawyer nearing the peak of his profession (in 1489, eleven years before his death, he was appointed presiding judge at the Cour des Aides), the tapestry was an expression of his aristocratic ambitions. The elaborate iconography contrasts the pleasures of the senses – sight, hearing, taste, smell, touch – with spiritual asceticism. In *Taste*, a monkey is about to bite into some delicacy or other, while the *134* lady is picking another out of the chalice. In *Hearing* the lady is playing *135* the organ while her servant operates the bellows. *Sight* is represented by the captured unicorn looking at its reflection in a mirror held by the lady. In *Smell*, a monkey is sniffing at a carnation while the lady is weaving a wreath of flowers. And *Touch* shows the lady delicately holding the unicorn's horn. The title of the sixth piece in the series, *'A mon seul désir'*, *116, 136* is clarified by the gesture of the lady, as she replaces her jewels in the casket proffered to her by her servant, indicating that in choosing her life-style, she is able to resist the pleasures of the senses. The painter (undoubtedly a great artist, and most likely French, given the artistic context of the late fifteenth century) succeeds in exploiting to the full the decorative potential of the *mille-fleurs* motif: clumps of small flowers adorn the island, and individual blossom-laden stalks are scattered across the background. The artist introduces all kinds of creatures, both familiar (fox, *137–139* sheep, partridge) and exotic (lion, panther, leopard), thus reviving the genre of tapestry known as *verdure*. The harmony of colours, with its innovative contrasting of red background and dark-blue islands, adds to the enchantment. The workmanship, in wool and silk, is proficient but not exceptional, and can be identified as that of a workshop in Paris or the Southern Netherlands.The combination of highly refined figures and realistic detail creates a very special poetic atmosphere.

With this unique range of hangings, including the famous *Lady and the Unicorn*, the Museum boasts one of the world's most significant collections of medieval tapestries.

V.H.

139 *The Lady and the Unicorn: Taste* (detail)

Everyday Life in the Late Middle Ages

From the time it was founded, the Museum took an interest not only in art but also in all the practical aspects of medieval civilization. As a result, it is now able to provide a full account of everyday life – how people lived, dressed, and ate – particularly at the end of the Middle Ages, for which evidence is more abundant. Of course, there is a considerable gap between the life of the peasant and that of the warrior or aristocrat. None the less, it is possible to give a diversified picture of medieval society – at least as it appears through the distorting prism of works of art, most of which were made for powerful people and thus reflect the social status quo rather than any opposition to it.

Housing, Furniture, and Everyday Objects

A large number of objects are available which make it possible to re-create the first 'wrapping' of everyday life, namely the medieval house – of which the Hôtel de Cluny provides a consummate aristocratic example. The doors to a house might be decorated with elaborate scenes that made the visitor aware of the owner's level of education and aspirations. Floor-tiles re-created in ceramic the air of natural greenery that had prevailed when the ground was strewn with flowers and foliage. Strangely, this decorative and illusionist trend was popularized by Cistercian monks, who were amongst the first to produce the two-colour tiling. The Museum has the good fortune to own a set of tiles that come either from Fontenay abbey or from the nearby château at Montbard. The fact that *141* either provenance is possible indicates that Cistercian art was popular not only because of its strict, untramelled style, but also because of the modular character of its designs, which could be transposed from one branch of art to another, from one place or domain to another.
The Museum's stock of furniture is such that it has actually been possible to re-create an entire late medieval room. This is decorated with secular *144* tapestries whose *mille-fleurs* design echoes the greenery – either real or ce- *126* ramic – which adorned the floor. Like the tapestries, which, by their nature, are movable and adaptable, the items of furniture are generally transportable and dismountable. The chest provides the most common form of storage, and tables are mounted on trestles, or may even fold down, as does the unique and particularly sophisticated example preserved in the Museum. Chests may be decorated in a great variety of ways: with tracery or carving in low relief, or, more rarely, with marquetry, or again with leather coverings and metal hinges – as is the case with the *coffre-bahut.* This type of container was particularly well suited to transportation, and several examples of it exist. The carved design in reserve is a speciality of the region around the Adige in northern Italy,

140 Stamping-die depicting
a knightly combat (detail)
France, 1st half 13th century
Stone

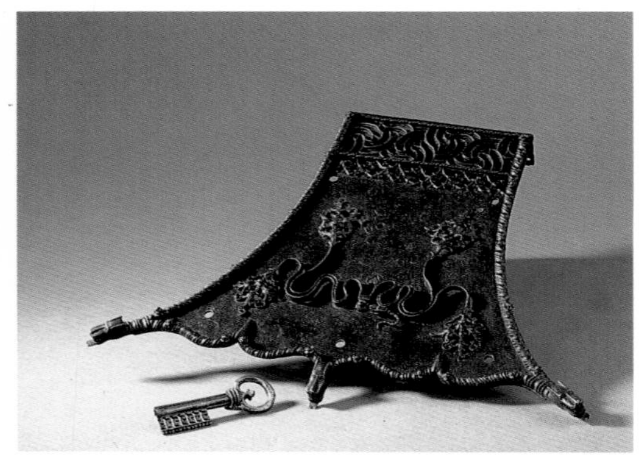

141 Floor-tiles from the abbey at Fontenay
France, 13th century
Ceramic with intaglio decoration

142 Bolt-lock and key
Germany, 15th century
Iron

143 Aquamanile in the shape
of a bust of a young man
Northern Germany
(Hildesheim?), early 14th century
Bronze

44 Plying table
France, 1480–1500
Wood

Coffre-bahut
France, 15th century
Wood, leather

Chest
Northern Italy, late 15th century
Wood marquetry, ivory, and stained bone

Aquamanile in the shape of a horse
Lower Saxony, 14th century
Bronze

Jug
France, 16th century
Pewter

Goblet
France (?), 14th century
Pewter

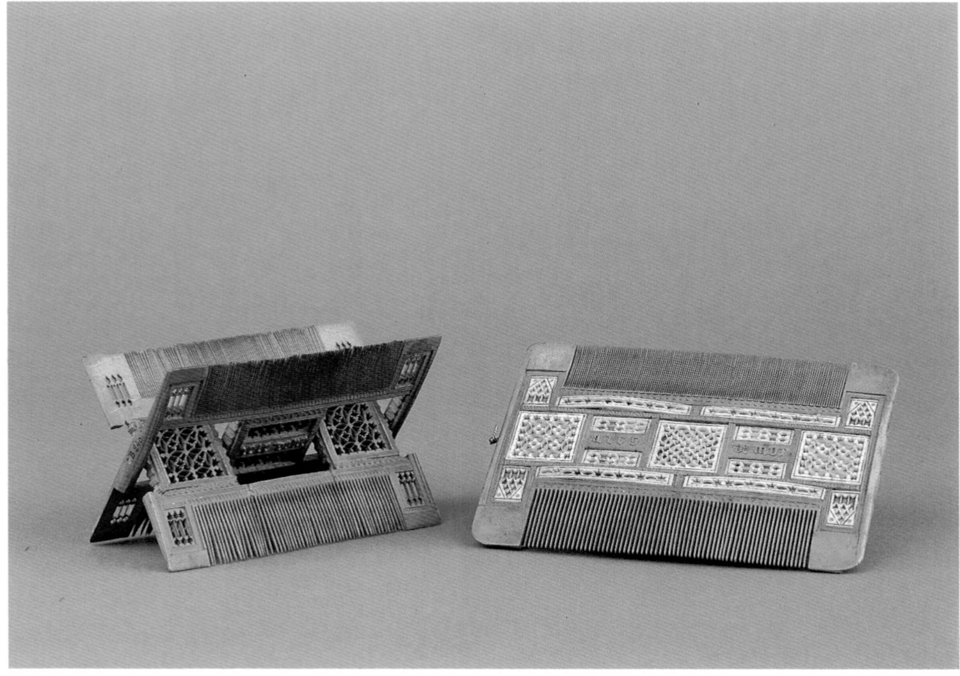

145 Jug
France (?), 14th–15th century
Bronze

Flame-decorated pot
Paris, 14th century
Ceramic

146 Two combs
France, *c.* 1500
Wood

which produced chests of a more luxurious kind, probably as wedding items, as is suggested by the Cluny example, with its amorous iconography and its space for a painted coat of arms. All these kinds of chests, as well as doors, shutters, and caskets, were equipped with bolts, locks, and keys. The great quantity of these which has come down to us does, it is true, indicate a desire for security – a very understandable concern in the unsettled times of the late Middle Ages; but it also betrays a need for privacy, contrary to the far too widespread notion of all-pervading communal life in the Middle Ages. *142*

In the reconstructed room are several objects reminding us of the variety of materials from which tableware might be made, depending on the rank of its owner or on whether it had a truly functional or purely decorative use. An aquamanile – the name may be roughly translated as 'water for hand-washing' – was a receptacle in which guests could wash their hands, and it was mostly a German speciality. The horse-shaped example in the Museum was produced in Lower Saxony, by a workshop whose name – 'the workshop of the lions with flame-shaped tails' – is sufficient to indicate the expressive style that characterized it. In contrast, an aquamanile in the shape of the bust of a young man, perhaps from Hildesheim, also in Lower Saxony, is a highly refined and unruffled piece of work. It must have been a luxury item, as would seem to be confirmed by the fact that it formed a pair with another aquamanile in the shape of the bust of a woman, now to be found in Moravia. These objects were used before the ritual of the repast began, and they give an indication of the rules of hygiene and hospitality of the time. During the Middle Ages there was a whole range of utensils for hand-washing, a custom that is a crucial feature of hospitality in all civilizations (and of liturgical ceremonial). There was also an important hygiene-related aspect to the ritual, since food was eaten with the hands. Hispano-Moorish pottery also includes some deep bowls which may have been used for this purpose. In contrast, a pewter jug (discovered when the church in Avioth, Lorraine, was restored) and a goblet have a more everyday character. Tableware of the more modest kind in wood, and of the more luxurious kind in glass, has rarely survived, and so a three-footed jug in bronze may perhaps be regarded as falling somewhere between the two. Although produced by quasi-industrial techniques, and although very simple in design, it nevertheless displays a certain degree of refinement in its animal-shaped spout and bevelled edge. A large-bellied pot reminds us of the omnipresence of ceramic in medieval civilization; it is one of the prime ingredients in archeological excavations, not only quantitatively but also in terms of the clues it can provide. This particular example is typical of everyday Parisian output in the fourteenth century, with its flame decoration and lack of glaze; the technique is also typical. With holes in the walls allowing air to circulate, the pot was reused to burn coal, which was believed to purify the air and offer protection against infections. This kind of item was used at funerals. The humble pot accompanied the deceased person to their resting-place, or else was reused in building foundations – which is where this particular one was discovered in the nineteenth century. *143* *145*

Very few items of clothing have come down to us, because the materials of which they were made mostly have not survived the ravages of time. We therefore have to turn to works of art to get some idea – even if only a rough one – of the way people dressed. Accessories, which were made of more durable materials, have fared better. Indispensable items of

147 Comb depicting the Annunciation
Italy, late 15th century
Ivory

148 Fragment of casket depicting
Orpheus charming the wild beasts
France, 14th century
Pewter

149 Casket depicting the Childhood of Christ and secular scenes
France, 15th century
Leather

Casket with image of Saint Apollonia
France, *c.* 1500
Iron, woodcut

female toilette such as combs and mirrors are decorated either with heraldic designs, amorous mottos (such as 'Ayes de moi merci' – 'Have mercy on me' – on a box-wood comb made in northern France), religious motifs (like the Annunciation on an ivory Italian comb), or courtly scenes (like the depiction of the court of the god of love on the leaf of an ivory Parisian box-mirror). But it is above all the caskets, used for a variety of purposes, which reveal the spread of courtly culture to ever wider circles. Their designs are perfectly matched to their purpose. Many are thought to have been lover's gifts or engagement presents – *Minnekästchen*, to use the Germanic term. Of course, it is not always possible to tell which of these objects were used to store toiletry items or jewellery and which were put to other, less poetic, uses – for example, as strong-

146

147

150

150 Leaf of box-mirror depicting courtly scenes
Paris, 1st half 14th century
Ivory

boxes for documents or cash. A fragment of casket shows Orpheus charming the wild beasts – one of many indications of the survival of classical culture in the Middle Ages. A large casket in leather has on it a combination of secular and religious scenes: Saints Stephen and Sebastian are shown flanking scenes from the childhood of Christ, whereas the other side features centaurs and putti engaging in fierce combats, while musicians, fools, and jugglers indulge in frenzied dancing. Such paradoxical juxtaposition is common in this late medieval period. The world is viewed as one, and it does not seem odd to anyone that a sacred picture should have a secular tinge to it, or vice versa. Hence the difficulty

148

149

in identifying the exact function of the large number of iron caskets, dating from about 1500, decorated with religious engravings – water-coloured woodcuts depicting scenes from the life of Christ and of the Virgin. Although these may have been a kind of alms-boxes, the picture on which was intended to appeal to the generosity of the faithful, they may equally well have been made for merchants and other travellers who wanted to entrust their souls – and their possessions? – into the care of an effective patron saint such as Saint Apollonia.

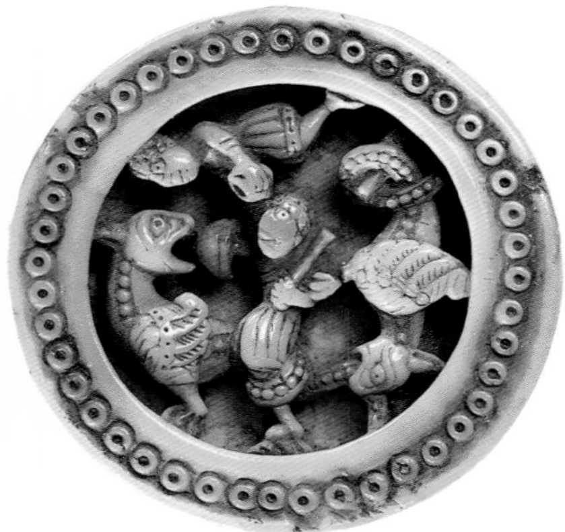

151 Shield depicting David and Goliath
Bohemia, *c.* 1480
Paint on wood, canvas, and leather

152 Backgammon piece depicting Hercules fighting the Hydra of Lerna
Northern Europe, 2nd half 12th century
Walrus tusk

Orders and Disorder in Society

As has already been indicated, it is not possible to match up all the everyday accessories with a single ideal medieval human being. The main source of commissions for secular objects was undoubtedly the fighting man, whose strength conferred on him unassailable power and riches. These individuals ranged in importance from princes to petty nobles. When not engaged in real warfare, the medieval knight spent his time jousting or competing in tournaments: the dividing-line between the two domains was, in any case, by no means a hard-and-fast one. The *140* military dress on a stamping-die preserved in the Museum indicates a date in the thirteenth century, the heyday of the aristocracy that fought in both Eastern crusades and Western wars. The reverse bears an engraving of a deer hunt – another favourite pastime of the noble classes. A *151* late fifteenth-century Bohemian shield depicts a youthful David in shepherd's garb (note the shepherd's crook in the left hand) ranged against the giant Goliath decked out in the weapons and armour of the day. Bundled up in his plate armour, sword on thigh and spear in hand, the giant is pictured with only his face emerging from an open-visored sallett. But armour was not the only distinguishing feature of the aristocratic classes. From Roman times, leisure was a sign of nobility, and indulging in games, even if this was a pursuit common to all classes in the Middle Ages, was nevertheless a means of displaying one's wealth and status. In the twelfth century, only a knight could have owned a set of *153* walrus-tusk counters for playing backgammon – one of the favourite board-games of the medieval period. The example in the Museum, with *152* its sophisticated mythological motif (Hercules fighting the Hydra of Lerna and another monster, aided by his companion Iolaus) is further evidence that this item was owned by someone from the cultured circles of the military aristocracy. Such games of strategy also reminded fighting men of real army expeditions and hard-fought one-to-one combat. This was probably also the reason for the success of a new board-game – *153* chess. It was introduced into the West around the year 1000, and its pieces, which were adapted from the Oriental originals, reflected contemporary social structures (king, queen, bishop, knight, pawn, etc.). And yet, by the end of the Middle Ages, the social order had been largely disrupted, as an aristocracy based on wealth grew up alongside, and indeed ousted, that based on military accomplishment. A very rare *153* games-box, unique in the number of games that can be played on it, was probably made for a well-to-do middle-class family.

But the most important order in medieval society was that of the clerics. They have already made many an appearance in this text, because it was mainly they who commissioned and used the religious objects which make up the great majority of surviving medieval works. But they are of dual interest to us at this particular point. In the first place, a number of

153 Games box
France (?), *c.* 1500
Ebony and stained walnut

Chess-pieces: King and Bishop
Scandinavia, early 14th century
Whale tusk

Backgammon piece depicting
a knight riding a cock
Northern Europe,
2nd half 12th century
Narwhal tusk

154 Mould for hosts depicting scenes from the Childhood of Christ
France, 2nd half 13th century
Iron

objects offer evidence of continual interaction between the sacred and the profane. A church door-knocker, for example, besides fulfilling its inherent function, was the means by which any layperson might seek the Church's protection and, in particular, benefit from the right to asylum. Furthermore, it was in the religious domain that mechanical reproduction processes and the idea of turning out multiple versions of works of art first emerged, and these were developments that played a crucial role in determining the functions and overall significance of art. Moulds or matrices with which it was possible to produce large numbers of a partic-

155

ular objects had always existed. These included moulds for making hosts, of which the Museum owns a rare early example of exceptional size. It is not hard to imagine the care that went into a work of this kind, given that it was to be used to produce the most important item in Christian ritual, and given that its size meant that the message it carried was highly visible. But besides this type of work – which, after all, was mostly the preserve of the clerical élite – there were the souvenirs called for by pilgrimages to provide evidence of their journeys and also to sustain their daily devotion once they were back home. A badge from Saint-Léonard-de-Noblat, for example, comes from a famous place of pilgrimage: as well as freeing possessed souls from the bonds of the devil, Saint Leonard delivered prisoners from their very real chains. Humble objects such as this, which were worn on clothing and sometimes accompanied their owners to the grave, were cast in lead, in order to keep the price low. The casting was done in stone moulds, of which the Museum owns a remarkable collection. The badges themselves were thus produced in their millions and are one of the chief aids in studying mass-produced images and the various nuances of medieval iconography long before the invention of engraving and printing.

154 *156*

In the Middle Ages, the third social order – that of the labourers – em-

156 Pilgrim's badge from Saint-Léonard-de-Noblat
France, 1st half 14th century
Lead

157 Coins from the Colmar treasury
Middle Rhineland, mid-14th century
Silver, gold

155 Door-knocker in the shape of a lion's head
Germany, 14th century
Bronze

braced mainly the rural classes; urban work and craft-based occupations took second place to agricultural production. It therefore goes without saying that any kind of trading or work with money was held in even less esteem. The almost universal condemnation of money-lenders and pawnbrokers was frequently accompanied by an anti-Semitism that sprang from other sources. The treasure found at Colmar, which, in addition to various coins, also contained a number of items of jewellery, including a Jewish wedding-ring, may have been buried at the time of the great persecutions. These were particularly marked in the Rhineland, following the Black Death which struck the West in the mid-fourteenth century. Peasants, meanwhile, are very often known only through the prism of the powerful classes. In a tapestry of the *Grape Harvest*, for example, the furrowed, almost caricature-like faces of the grape-pickers contrast with the fine, distinguished features of the seigneurial owners of the vineyard. As regards scenes depicting work in the fields, they do, it is true, provide a very lively image, but it is a stereotyped one – as, for example, in a misericord illustrating the killing of a pig.

157 *107* *158, 127* *160*

160 Misericord depicting the killing of a pig (detail)
Burgundy (?), end 14th century
Wood

159 Misericord depicting a pig playing the organ
Eastern France (?), 15th century
Wood

158 *The Grape Harvest* (detail)
Southern Netherlands, early 16th century
Tapestry in wool and silk

But mockery does also go on in medieval society – perhaps offering an 'upside down' picture of the world. Misericords often also provided an opportunity of engaging in lively satire, and were perfectly placed to do so, given their hidden position under monks' and canons' seats. Misericords were small ledges on which the members of the religious community could lean during long religious services, many of which were conducted standing. In contrast to the overall iconography of the stalls, which relates to serious sacred themes, that of the misericords offered an opportunity of relating some comical tales, or of illustrating humorous proverbs, or even of lampooning the clergy and making fun of the dignity of their office – as in the picture of a pig playing the organ. If one remembers that the individuals commissioning the stalls were the same ones that sat on them, it becomes clear just how much humour and self-mockery, and even rather wild letting-off of steam there must have been during the Middle Ages. This was a much-needed counterbalance to the constant striving towards the divine which, in deed or word, was the only ultimate objective of this highly religious society. *159*

P.-Y.L.P.

Index and Bibliography

Italics refer to illustrations

Names

Abelard, Peter 34
Alençon, Pierre d' 50
Alexander VI, Pope 75
Alphonse de Poitiers 50
Amboise, Jacques d' 9
Areobindus, consul *16*, 19

Baillet, Jean 103
Bar, Countess of *94*, 95
Bataille, Nicolas 98
Baudouin of Flanders 79
Beauneveu, André 53
Billant, Pierre du 97
Burgundy, Dukes of 53, 68, 98

Campin, Robert 103
Carjat *10*
Charlemagne 23
Charles IV, German Emperor 89
Charles V, King of France 96
Charles VI, King of France 68, 98
Charles VII, King of France 72, *72*
Clovis 23
Constantine, Roman Emperor 13, 14

Daret, Jacques 103
Deutz, Rupert of 35
Devéria, Achille 9, *9*
Dürer, Albrecht 99
Du Sommerard, Alexandre *7*, 9, *9*, 10, 11, 78
Du Sommerard, Edmond *10*, 11, 97, 98, 111

Edward III, King of England 94
Ermengarde, Countess *94*, 95
Etex, Antoine *11*
Eudoxia, Byzantine princess 27
Eyck, Barthélemy d' 97, *98*

Fleckenstein, Family 70
Flouri, Guillaume de 82, *82*
Fouquet, Jean 72, *72*
François I, King of France 9

Geiler, Hans 61, *61*
Geoffroy-Dechaume, Adolphe-Victor 50
Gregory VII, Pope 31
Greiff, Hanns *91*
Gyrard, Laurent 72

Hellande, Guillaume de 103
Hemmel, Peter 70, *70*
Heinrich II, German Emperor 27

Imola, Benvenuto d' 72, *72*
Isabel of Bavaria 98
Isabelle de France 50

Jean de Liège 53
Jean II le Bon, King of France 87
John XXII, Pope 85, 94
Jean sans Peur 68
Jeanne de Bourbon, Queen of France 96
Jeanne de Toulouse 50, *50*
Jouvenel des Ursins, Family *70*, 70
Julian the Apostate, Roman Emperor *8*, 14, *15*
Julien, Guillaume *84*, 85

Lakanal, Joseph 47
Lannoy, Robert de *51*, 53
Lenoir, Albert 10, *11*
Lenoir, Alexandre 9
Le Viste, Jean 111
Limburg brothers 72
Louis d'Orléans, 98
Louis VI, King of France 35
Louis IX (Saint Louis), King of France 50, 67, 79, 80, 82
Louis XII, King of France 75
Ludwig of Bavaria, German Emperor 85
Lusignan, Hugues de 82

Master Arnt 56, *58*
Master E.S. 70
Master of Riofrio 75, *75*
Manassès, Count *94*, 95
Marguerite de Provence 50
Meissonier, Jean 50
Mérimée, Prosper 9, 111
Montaigu, Gérard de 68, *68*
Montreuil, Pierre de *50*, 50
Muret, Etienne de 40

Nalduccio, Angelo di *57*
Nicomachi 14, *16*, 19
Nourriche, Guillaume de 53

Otto II, German Emperor 27, *28*

Philippe IV le Bel, King of France 50, 85
Pigouchet, Philippe 75
Poissonier, Arnold 98
Pucelle, Jean 67, 68

Quarton, Enguerrand 72

René d'Anjou, Count of Provence 97
Robert, Hubert 7
Rudolf of Nidau, Count 85, *87*
Roman II, Byzantine Emperor 27

Sand, George 111
Schongauer, Martin 70
Siena, Minucchio da 85, *87*
Sluter, Claus 53
Soufflot, Germain 47
Suger, abbot 35
Symmachi 14, *16*

Theodosius, Roman Emperor 14
Theophanu, Byzantine princess 27, *28*
Tiberius, Roman Emperor 14

Vacquer, Théodore 7
Van der Weyden, Roger 72
Vannini, Pietro *87*
Varie, Simon de 72
Verdun, Nicolas de 43
Via, Arnaud de *93*, 94
Viollet-le-Duc, Eugène 47, 50
Voragine, Jacobus de 103

Werve, Claus de 53
Wibald, abbot 38

Places

Abbeville 75, *75*
Aachen 20
Amiens 75
Angers 23, 31, 98
Antwerp 61, *62*, 72, 95
Aragon 87
Arras 96, *97*, 99
Aulnay 31
Auvergne *43*, 68
Auxerre 103, *104*
Averbode (Belgium) 61
Avignon 85, 94
Avioth 117

Basle 11, *26*, 27, 85
Bamberg (Germany) *26*, 27
Barcelona (Spain) 87, *89*
Beauvais 80, 103
Besançon 19
Betton *69*, 70
Bohemia *88*, 89, *120*
Bologna (Italy) 56, *56*
Boussac 111
Brussels 38, *63*, 99
Burgundy 9, *55*, 95, *125*

Castelsagrat *24*
Castile *75*
Catalonia *45*, 55, 87
Châlons-sur-Marne 89, *91*
Champmol 53
Charlieu 43, *43*
Chartres 35, 55
Chinon 93
Cluny 9
Colmar 67, 85, *85*, *123*, 125
Cologne (Germany) 27, *28*, 89, 94
Constantinople *16*, 19, *20*, 20, 27, 79

Dendermonde (Belgium) *77*
Dijon *53*

Echternach (Luxemburg) *13*, 27
Egypt 19, *19*, *21*, 23, 77, 93, 98
England *27*, *28*, *32*

Flanders 77, 78, 79, 93, 98, 99
Florence (Italy) 93, 94
Fontenay 113, *114*
Fribourg (Switzerland) *61*

Gaul *23*, 23
Genoa (Italy) 94, 103
Gercy 50, 65, *66*
Garona (Catalonia) 43
Gloucester (England) 31
Grandmont 40, *41*
Guarrazar (Spain) 23, *24*

Hildesheim (Germany) *38*, 117
Huysburg (Germany) 38, *43*, 94

Ingolstadt (Germany) *91*
Italy 9, 23, *32*, 34, 43, 55, 56, 68, 72, 79, *82*, 85, 87, 93, *93*, 94, *115*, *117*

Kalkar (Germany) 56, *58*
Koblenz (Germany) 38

Lavaudieu 43
Le Puy 43
Liège (Belgium) 38
Lille 99
Limoges 40, *40*, *41*, 43, 78, *78*, 79, *79*, *80*
Longchamp *52*, 53
Luccà (Italy) 19, 93, *93*

Metz 31, *32*
Montbard 113
Moravia (Tchech Rep.) 117
Moûtiers-en-Tarentaise 77, *77*

Normandy *63*, 67
Nottingham (England) *61*, 61
Novara (Italy) *32*, 34

Paris, Hôtel de Cluny 7, *7*, 9, 75, *75*, 113
Paris, Cluny Baths 7
Paris, Notre-Dame 14, 35, *37*, 43, 47, *47*, *48*, 50, 70, 80,
Paris, Sainte-Chapelle 43, *45*, 50, *51*, 66, *66*, 67, 79, 80, 93, 95, 96
Paris, Sainte-Geneviève 34, *35*
Paris, Saint-Germain-des-Prés 34, *34*, 50, *50*, 93
Poissy 50, *51*
Prussia *58*

Rhineland *58*, *85*, *99*, *123*, 125
Rome 13, *16*, 19, 23, 103,
Rouen 67, *67*, 98

Saint-Amand 35
Saint-Denis 31, *31*, 34, 35, *37*, 43, 50, 67
Saint-Léonard-de-Noblat 123, *123*
Saint-Marc-le-Blanc *13*
Saint-Mihiel 95
Saint-Omer 35, 38
Saint-Sulpice *82*
Scandinavia *121*
Siena (Italy) *57*, 93
Southern Netherlands 99, 111, *125*
Spain *22*, *24*, *41*
Stavelot (Belgium) 38
Strasbourg *70*
Suffolk (England) *65*, 68

Tarascon 72, *73*
Toledo (Spain) 23
Tuscany *54*, 56
Toulouse *22*, 23, 50, 93
Tournai (Belgium) 98, 99, *103*
Tours 97
Tressan *24*
Troyes 43, *45*

Venice (Italy) 94, 95
Vergy 95
Vézelay 43
Villefranche-sur-Saône *69*, 70

Bibliography

Adam, Jean-Pierre and Delhumeau, Herveline, *Les thermes antiques de Lutèce*. Paris, Réunion des Musées Nationaux, forthcoming (1996).

Antoine, Elisabeth, *Le Tour du musée en 80 œuvres*. Paris, Réunion des Musées Nationaux, 1995.

Bruna, Denis, *Enseignes de pèlerinage et enseignes profanes au musée national du Moyen Age*. Paris, Réunion des Musées Nationaux, forthcoming (1996).

Caillet, Jean-Pierre, *L'Antiquité classique, le Haut Moyen Age et Byzance au musée de Cluny*. Paris, Réunion des Musées Nationaux, 1985.

Erlande-Brandenburg, Alain, *La Dame à la licorne*. Paris, Réunion des Nationaux, 1989.

Erlande-Brandenburg, Alain, *Les Sculptures de Notre-Dame de Paris au musée de Cluny*. Paris, Réunion des Musées Nationaux, 1982.

Erlande-Brandenburg, Alain, *Les Statues de Notre-Dame de Paris*. Paris, Réunion des Musées Nationaux (Petits Guides, No. 109).

Erlande-Brandenburg, Alain, Le Pogam, Pierre-Yves, and Sandron, Dany, *Musée national du moyen Age – Thermes de Cluny – Guide to the collections*. Paris, Réunion des Musées Nationaux, 1993.

Joubert, Fabienne, *La Tapisserie médiévale au musée de Cluny*. Paris, Réunion des Musées Nationaux, 1987.

Klagsbald, Victor, *Catalogue raisonné de la collection juive du musée de Cluny*. Paris, Réunion des Musées Nationaux, 1981.

Le Pogam, Pierre-Yves, *Musée national du Moyen Age – Thermes de Cluny*. Paris, Réunion des Musées Nationaux, 1994 (Petits Guides, No. 3).

Lorquin, Alexandra, *Les Tissus coptes du musée national du Moyen Age – Thermes de Cluny. Etoffes de lin et de laine*. Paris, Réunion des Musées Nationaux, 1992.

Sandron, Dany, *Roman et premier art gothique: la sculpture de XIe et XIIe siècles au musée national du Moyen Age*. Paris, Réunion des Musées Nationaux, forthcoming.

Taburet-Delahaye, Elisabeth, *Les Ivoires de Cluny*. Paris, Réunion des Musées Nationaux (Petits Guides, No. 79).

Taburet-Delahaye, Elisabeth, *L'Orfèvrerie gothique (XIIIe – début XVe s.) au musée de Cluny*. Paris, Réunion des Musées Nationaux, 1989.